Corporate Acquisitions and Mergers in Hungary

Corporate Acquisitions and Mergers in Hungary

Second Edition

Áron Barta
Szabolcs Szilágyi

Kinstellar

Katalin Banász
Agnes Szabo

Becher & Torma

This book was originally published as a chapter in Corporate Acquisitions and Mergers.

General Editor: Peter Begg

Wolters Kluwer

Published by:
Kluwer Law International B.V.
PO Box 316
2400 AH Alphen aan den Rijn
The Netherlands
E-mail: lrs-sales@wolterskluwer.com
Website: www.wolterskluwer.com/en/solutions/kluwerlawinternational

Sold and distributed by:
Wolters Kluwer Legal & Regulatory U.S.
920 Links Avenue
Landisville, PA 17538
United States of America
E-mail: customer.service@wolterskluwer.com

ISBN 978-94-035-3098-7

e-Book: ISBN 978-94-035-3108-3
web-PDF: ISBN 978-94-035-3118-2

Contents

Kinstellar

Kinstellar is a leading independent law firm in Emerging Europe, Turkey and Central Asia, with offices in Almaty and Nur-Sultan (Kazakhstan), Belgrade (Serbia), Bratislava (Slovakia), Bucharest (Romania), Budapest (Hungary), Istanbul (Turkey), Kyiv (Ukraine), Prague (the Czech Republic), Sofia (Bulgaria) and Tashkent (Uzbekistan), but operating as a single fully integrated firm, offering consistently high-quality services across all jurisdictions in an integrated and seamless style.

The Budapest-based Hungarian team of Kinstellar has been working together since 2000 and handling some of Hungary's most significant transactions. With the office's extensive experience, the lawyers combine first-class legal skills with an in-depth understanding of business objectives while providing top-quality client service to international and domestic investors active across a range of industry sectors, including automotive, aviation, banking and financial services, energy and utilities, food and beverages, manufacturing, mining, real estate and telecommunications.

The M&A service of Kinstellar Budapest works as an integrated team, combining M&A expertise with bespoke sector-specific advice, with a specific emphasis on M&A in the banking and finance, energy, TMT, life sciences and healthcare, and real estate sectors. Our lawyers are also adept at advising on complex corporate restructurings, including demergers and domestic and cross-border mergers.

Each service of Kinstellar Budapest has been consistently ranked in various legal directories (Legal 500, Chambers Global, Chambers Europe and IFRL1000) as one of the first choices in Hungary for their core areas and all our partners are singled out in the top categories.

Authors

Áron Barta is a Senior Associate in the Corporate practice in Budapest.

He focuses on Corporate, Capital Markets and Corporate Restructuring matters. His expertise encompasses capital market matters including IPOs and SPO and he has experience advising and representing leading multinational corporates in handling the wide range of legal, regulatory and strategic issues arising from complex corporate restructuring projects. He has also experience in advising other corporate and financial regulatory questions.

Áron completed his law studies at Eötvös Loránd University, Budapest and in the frame of Erasmus programme, he studied law at the Université de Poitiers. He speaks Hungarian, English and French.

Szabolcs Szilágyi is an Associate in the Budapest office and a member of the employment & labour law team.

His main focus is employment law, with particular emphasis on drafting documentation for establishing and terminating employment relationships, providing strategic advice and assistance in relation to the terminations and advising on employment aspects of corporate acquisitions and disposals.

Szabolcs completed his law studies at the University of Debrecen and studied EU Law at the Hogeschool Utrecht University. He speaks Hungarian and English.

Becher & Torma

Becher & Torma is a boutique tax advisory firm providing premium tax services in Hungary. Although being an independent tax advisory firm, B&T regularly works together with international law firms and tax advisory firms in cross-border and domestic transactions. Most of the senior team members joined from market-leading advisory firms (the Big4), high-end international law firms or the Hungarian Ministry of Finance who developed extensive expertise in various areas of tax law and tax advisory services.

Authors

Katalin Banász joined B&T in 2021 as a tax manager. She has economics degrees majoring in accounting from Budapest Business School, College of Finance and Accountancy and Budapest University of Technology and Economics. Katalin is a certified tax advisor, and she also has an accountant qualification. She has previously gained experience in tax compliance and tax advisory matters both at advisory firms and corporate side.

Agnes Szabo joined Becher, Torma and Partners Law Firm as a junior lawyer in 2022. She completed her law studies at Pázmány Péter Catholic University of Budapest. During her university studies, Ágnes gained experience at Becher, Torma and Partners Law Firm as a trainee in 2020.

Tax part of this chapter has been updated and revised by Becher & Torma tax advisors.

1 ECONOMIC, POLITICAL AND CULTURAL FACTORS

1.1 Geography

[01] Hungary is situated in Central Europe and occupies an area of 93 030 sq. km. Hungary is bordered by Slovakia to the north, Ukraine and Romania to the east, Serbia and Croatia to the south, Slovenia to the southwest and Austria to the west. The country's capital and largest city is Budapest.

[02] The majority of the landscape consists of plains and low mountains. Hungary's geography has traditionally been defined by its two main waterways, the Danube and Tisza rivers, which are both navigable. The Balaton, the largest lake in Central Europe, can also be found in Hungary. Natural treasures of the country include the arable land and the waterways. The latter includes a number of high-quality artesian springs and various types of thermal springs. Hungary is a popular tourist destination, with total foreign tourist guest nights spent in the country surpassing 15.7 m in the year 2019, but unfortunately with a year-on-year decline of about 75% in the year 2020 due to the COVID-19 pandemic.

1.2 Population

[03] The population of Hungary has been declining steadily since 2001. According to the census of 2022, the total population of Hungary was 9 603 634. Bringing the population decrease to a halt is a primary government objective, with many financial incentives provided for families to increase the birth rate, however, the age pyramid still depicts an ageing population. More than one-quarter of the population lives in the Budapest Metropolitan area.

[04] The official language is Hungarian, and the currency is the Hungarian Forint (HUF).

[05] Approximately 74.7% of the population active in the labour market (i.e., the age group between 15–64 years) is employed. The unemployment rate in December 2023 was 4.2%. Low-skilled labour demand in certain sectors now exceeds the supply, The education system and outcomes are relatively good on average, although it has shortcomings due to the relatively low salaries in the sector and the lack of new teachers. Generalized homeownership is an obstacle to the mobility of the labour force.

1.3 Transport

[06] Hungary has a highly developed road, railway, air and water transportation system, including a total length of approximately 2 076 km motorways, five international airports and a railroad system of 7 558 km. Budapest is directly connected to the Austrian, Slovakian, Romanian, Serbian, Croatian, and Slovenian borders via motorways. Due to its location and geographical features, several transport corridors cross Hungary.

1.4 Government and Political System

[07] Hungary is a democratic parliamentary republic, which is recognized today as a developed country and is politically stable. Hungary is a member of the European Union, the NATO, the OECD, the WTO, the Visegrád Group, and the Schengen Area.

[08] The economy of Hungary is a medium-sized, structurally, politically and institutionally open economy, which is a part of the European Union's single market and is generally open to foreign investors. Hungary is well-integrated into the global financial system and is a favourable environment for both foreign and domestic entrepreneurs.

1.5 Legal System

[09] Hungary is a civil law country. The Hungarian court system is independent and the legal background for the enforcement of contractual claims and other rights, as well as the operation of Hungarian courts, are well-established. Nevertheless, the courts are often overloaded, which, in addition to the multiple instance processes because of appeals, generally results in lengthy court proceedings (approximately two to three years long).

2 CURRENT ECONOMIC ASPECTS

[10] In a technical sense, the recession ended in the Hungarian economy in the third quarter of 2012, with GDP figures showing a steady increase, which is the result of, amongst other things, the introduction of a number of special taxes over recent years, which have helped bring the budget deficit below 3% of the GDP. At the same time, such special taxes have begun to undermine the predictability and simplicity of the tax system. The widespread use of public employment helps to keep the unemployment rate at a medium level.

[11] Growth potential is held back by weak investment in high-added value industries, salaries below the EU average and shortcomings in labour and product markets. Access to international bond markets has improved significantly, but the still high foreign currency indebtedness both in the public and the private sectors remains a key vulnerability. In order to give a boost to the economy, the Hungarian government offer various incentives for foreign investors.

[12] The war between Russia and Ukraine, and the globally increasing inflation resulted in a halt in the Hungarian economy. The economic growth was 4.6% in 2022, and the forecast for 2023 is –0.4%. Hungarian inflation rates were the highest within the EU (17.6%) in 2023. By the end of 2023 the recession is real GDP growth is forecast to pick up to 2.4% in 2024. The first estimate of GDP data for Q4 2023 is expected in February 2024.

3 MAIN INDUSTRIES

[13] The main sectors of the Hungarian industry are heavy industry (mining, metallurgy, machine and steel production), energy production, mechanical engineering, chemicals, food industry and automobile production. In recent years battery industry skyrocketed in Hungary, and numerous battery manufacturing, disassembling and waste management factories have been established/decided to be established. Hungary's main agricultural products are wheat, corn, sunflower seed, potatoes, sugar beet; pigs, cattle, poultry, and dairy products.

[14] The private sector accounts for more than 80% of the Hungarian GDP. Foreign ownership of and investment in Hungarian firms are widespread. The extent of state ownership in the Hungarian economy is expending in certain sectors (telecommunication, banking, insurance) as some companies have recently been acquired by the state, but overall is still low compared to the economy as a whole.

3.1 The M&A Market

[15] The M&A market performed well and had increased significantly until it was hit with the COVID-19 pandemic in 2020 but by 2022–2023 it had recovered. According to Ernst & Young's survey in 2022, there were 137 transactions in Hungary. The estimated value of the Hungarian M&A market was USD5.88 bn, which is a 27% growth compared to 2021. The average value of transactions under USD100 m was USD22 m. The most active sector was the IT sector. The number of state purchases is showing a significant increase.

3.2 Cultural Aspects

[16] According to professional international studies, the Hungarian economy is considered one of the most open economies internationally. Hungary was ranked in the 52nd place by the ease of doing business index published by the World Bank for 2020.

[17] Since 2012, the Hungarian government has entered into nearly ninety strategic agreements with foreign and Hungarian companies, including among others Coca-Cola, Daimler AG, Suzuki Hungary, Audi Hungary, GE Hungary, Tesco Hungary, GlaxoSmithKline, ExxonMobil, Nokia Siemens Networks, Roche and

Siemens. The aim of such strategic agreements is to create a stable environment for prominent companies to carry out their activities in Hungary while improving innovation, research and development and fostering the growth of the Hungarian economy and employment.

[18] Hungary is a moderately expensive place to do business. The consumer prices are relatively low (although there was a significant increase in food prices in the course of 2022–2023), as are local salaries. However, labour costs can be high because of the various taxes and statutory contributions.

[19] The giving and acceptance of gifts is not a normal feature of the day-to-day economy. Small gifts may be acceptable, but many middle-sized and large companies, especially those having an international background, have introduced anti-corruption policies regulating this issue. In December 2023, the Hungarian Government accepted a legislation proposal for a new law to criminalize the acceptance of foreign donations in case of a member/nominee/leader of a political party.

4 DEFINITIONS

[20] For the purposes of this summary, the following words and phrases shall have the meanings set out below:

- '*Bankruptcy Act*' means Act XLIX of 1991 on bankruptcy proceedings and liquidation proceedings.
- '*Capital Market Act*' means Act CXX of 2001 on Capital Market.
- '*Civil Code*' means Act V of 2013 on the Civil Code.
- '*Companies' Register*' means the register containing the data of Hungarian business enterprises as defined by section 10 of Act V of 2006 on public company information, company registration and winding-up proceedings.
- '*Competition Act*' means Act LVII of 1996 on the Prohibition of Unfair Trading Practices and Unfair Competition.
- '*Competition Authority*' or '*HCA*' means the Hungarian Competition Authority ('Gazdasági Versenyhivatal' or 'GVH').
- '*Court of Registration*' means the competent Hungarian county court or metropolitan court keeping the Companies' Register.
- '*Credit Institutions Act*' means Act CCXXXVII of 2013 on Credit Institutions and Financial Enterprises.
- '*Cross-border Transformation Act*' means Act CXL of 2007 on Cross-Border Mergers of Limited Liability Companies.
- '*Insurance Act*' means Act LXXXVIII of 2014 on Insurance Activities.
- '*Investment Service Providers Act*' means Act CXXXVIII of 2007 on Investment Firms and Commodity Dealers, and on the Regulations Governing their Activities.
- '*Labour Code*' means Act I of 2012 on the Labour Code.
- '*NAV*' means the Hungarian Tax and Customs Authority.
- '*Transformation Act*' means Act CLXXVI of 2013 on the Transformation, Merger and Division of Legal Entities.

5 THE REGULATORY FRAMEWORK

5.1 Business Vehicles

5.1.1 Available Corporate Structures

[21] The following main corporate forms are available in Hungary: limited liability company (*'korlátolt felelősségű társaság'* or *'Kft'.*); company limited by shares (*'részvénytársaság'* or *'Zrt.'/'Nyrt.'*); partnership (*'közkereseti társaság'* or *'Kkt.'*); and limited partnership (*'betéti tárasaság'* or *'Bt.'*). In addition, entrepreneurs are entitled to carry out business activities on a self-employed basis (*'egyéni vállalkozó'*), and cooperatives also exist as a special legal form. The formation of a European company limited by shares (*'Societas Europea'*) is also possible under Hungarian law albeit rarely used.

[22] Foreign entities may also conduct business in Hungary via a branch office, which may acquire rights and undertake obligations under its own business name, but for and on behalf of the foreign undertaking. However, a branch office may not establish or acquire ownership in a Hungarian company.

[23] Foreign entities may also establish their commercial representative offices in Hungary, but such entities qualify as the organizational units of a foreign company that is not involved in business activities in its own name, and the foreign entity is directly liable for the obligations of the representative office.

5.1.2 Compliance, Registration and Reporting Requirements

Companies' register

[24] All companies are required to be registered in the Companies' Register held by the respective Court of Registration. Registration takes one business day (when using pro forma documentation) or up to fifteen business days (in the case of the use of non-standardized documentation) from the date on which the tax number of the company was issued by the NAV as a result of the tax registration procedure. Nonetheless, a company is deemed to exist and may commence business activities upon the countersigning of its deed of incorporation by a lawyer or the inclusion thereof in a notarial deed.

[25] Documents that are to be submitted to the Companies' Register must be in the Hungarian language or translated into Hungarian by a certified translator.

[26] The most important data of companies is publicly available, online free of charge (www.e-cegjegyzek.hu). The deed of foundation, corporate resolutions and financial statements of companies are also accessible online to the general public upon the payment of certain fees.

Tax registration procedure

[27] When a company is established, the NAV conducts a tax registration procedure. In the course of the tax registration procedure, the NAV investigates whether there are any obstacles to the issuance of a tax number for the company. The NAV shall issue the tax number to the company under registration within one business day if no obstacle to the issuance of the tax number is likely to arise by this deadline. In any other case, the NAV will make its decision in respect of the issuance or rejection of the tax number within eight business days. The NAV informs the Court of Registration electronically if the tax number has not been issued within one business day. In such a case, the Court of Registration will suspend the company registration procedure until the date of the receipt of further notice from the NAV in respect of the tax number.

5.1.3 Most Common Corporate Vehicles

[28] The most common forms of company in Hungary in respect of large-scale businesses are limited liability companies and companies limited by shares, which are primarily used in corporate mergers and acquisitions. Both such company forms are equity-based and have registered capital that is contributed by the founders. They are both legal entities and the liability of their shareholders is limited (subject to a limited number of exemptions).

[29] As far as ownership structure is concerned, generally, both a limited liability company and a company limited by shares may have a sole member/shareholder, which may be either a natural person and/or a legal entity. Certain businesses can be established only in the form of a company that is limited by shares (e.g., in the financial services sector), and with an increased mandatory registered capital.

Limited liability company

(i) Basic characteristics

[30] A limited liability company is a vehicle generally used in situations in which there is a limited number of investors who plan to hold their investments in the company for the medium to long term. A limited liability company is typically used for relatively small- to medium-sized enterprises. A limited liability company may be founded by one or more members ('quotaholder(s)').

(ii) Foundation

[31] The founders established a limited liability company by the signing of the articles of association (or, in the case of a sole-member company, a deed of foundation). Such documents must be prepared and countersigned by a Hungarian lawyer or be in the form of a notarial deed.

(iii) Registered capital

[32] The minimum registered capital required for a limited liability company is HUF3 m (approximately EUR7 960). The registered capital of a limited liability company is divided into ownership interests (i.e., a business quota or '*üzletrész*').

Each member holds a business quota which corresponds to the percentage of its ownership in the limited liability company. Co-ownership of a business quota in a limited liability company is also possible. The business quota carries the rights and duties of each member, in particular voting rights and the right to dividends.

[33] The registered capital of a limited liability company and the capital contributions of individual members are recorded in the Companies' Register. Any changes to the registered capital must be approved by the members' meeting of the relevant limited liability company and recorded in the Companies' Register. Contributions to the registered capital of a limited liability company can be in the form of cash or in-kind contributions. The value of in-kind contributions is determined by the agreement of the members, or they may appoint an independent expert (e.g., auditor) for this task.

(iv) Corporate governance

[34] The main governing body of a limited liability company is the members' meeting. Decision-making may be implemented in person, via electronic devices, proxy votes or written circular resolutions.

[35] A limited liability company is managed and represented by one or more managing directors elected by the limited liability company's members' meeting. A limited liability company's deed of incorporation may limit the representation and management rights of a managing director, however, such limitations are not effective vis-à-vis third parties.

[36] While executing their tasks, managing directors are required to act with due care, giving priority to the interests of the company (as opposed to the interests of the members).

[37] Unless stipulated otherwise in the limited liability company's deed of incorporation, the managing director has, *inter alia*, the following competencies: (i) sole or joint representation of the company and management of operations of the company in accordance with the Civil Code, the deed of incorporation and any members' resolutions; (ii) establishing the business plan of the limited liability company; (iii) convening members' meetings and proposing the agenda thereof; and (iv) implementing the resolutions of the members' meeting.

(v) Pre-emption rights

[38] Statutory pre-emption rights apply in favour of the other members, the company itself or a third party appointed by the members' meeting (in that order), unless such right is excluded in the deed of incorporation of the limited liability company.

(vi) Other relevant issues

[39] In general, a limited liability company may, but is not required to, appoint an internal auditor and/or a supervisory board. However, the appointment of a supervisory board is mandatory if the number of employees exceeds 200, and the workers' council did not waive its right to delegate a supervisory board member. In addition, the appointment of an auditor is mandatory if: (i) the company's annual net sales exceeded a yearly average of HUF300 m over the two financial years preceding the financial year under review; and (ii) the average number of employees of the company over the two financial years preceding the financial year under review exceeded fifty persons.

Company limited by shares

(i) Basic characteristics and foundation

[40] Companies limited by shares (*'részvénytársaság'*) are established in Hungary normally where significant founding capital is required or if a specific regulation requires this company form (e.g., in the case of financial services or insurance activities).

[41] There are two types of companies limited by shares: private and public. In both cases, the liability of the shareholder is typically limited to the obligation to contribute to the registered capital.

[42] Under the Civil Code, a company limited by shares may only be founded as a private company limited by shares. Following the foundation, the company may then change its operational form and operate as a public company limited by shares. Only a few dozen public companies limited by shares operate in Hungary.

[43] In the case of both private and public companies limited by shares, the founders execute the company's deed of foundation. The company can legally operate as a pre-company from the date of the countersigning of its deed of foundation by a lawyer or the incorporation of the deed of foundation in a notarial deed.

(ii) Registered capital

[44] The registered capital of a company limited by shares is divided into a certain number of shares with a specified nominal value. The minimum registered capital is HUF5 m (approximately EUR13 270) for private and HUF20 m (approximately EUR53 000) for public companies limited by shares.

[45] Contributions to the registered capital of a company limited by shares can be in cash or in kind. The value of in-kind contributions must be certified by an auditor or verified by the recent annual report of the shareholder providing the contribution.

(iii) Shares

[46] The share certificates may be issued in the form of printed shares or de-materialized shares registered on a securities account.

[47] A company limited by shares is required to give equal treatment to all shareholders but may issue ordinary shares, various preference shares and/or employee shares.

[48] Typical preference share rights include preference over ordinary shares in dividend distributions, the right of first refusal over shares to be transferred, and priority in distribution of dividends in the event of the company's liquidation. Voting preference shares may also be issued, which may even result in a '*golden share*' preventing the adoption of a decision without the consent of the holders of such golden share or shares. A special preference share may entitle the shareholder to appoint or recall one or more members of the board of directors or supervisory board.

(iv) Corporate governance

[49] The main corporate organs of a company limited by shares are: (i) the general meeting; (ii) the board of directors (or general manager, in the case of a private company limited by shares); (iii) the supervisory board; and/or (iv) an internal auditor or audit committee (if any):

(a) General meeting: The general meeting of a company limited by shares is the supreme decision-making body of the company and may pass resolutions in person, via electronic devices, proxy vote or written circular resolutions.
(b) Board of directors or general manager: Either the board of directors (consisting of a minimum of three members) or the general manager is in charge of operational decisions and day-to-day management.
(c) Supervisory board: A supervisory board is mandatory only in the case of public companies limited by shares, but often operates also in private companies limited by shares.
The role of a supervisory board is to supervise the management on behalf of the shareholders. This is usually restricted to requesting information from the management and examining the financial statements before the approval of the general meeting.
However, the supervisory board may play a more significant role in the organization, as further competencies might be allotted to the supervisory board in addition to its mandatory tasks. For example, the deed of foundation may authorize the supervisory board to exercise certain rights normally belonging to the competence of the general meeting, such as the election and removal of executive officers and the approval of certain transactions.
(d) Auditor committee: A public company limited by shares is also required to have an audit committee which assists the management of the company and the supervisory board in the supervision of the financial report regime, the selection of the auditor and cooperation with the auditor.
Auditor: Companies limited by shares are required to have an auditor; however, in the case of a private company limited by shares the shareholders may waive this requirement in the deed of foundation.

(v) Transfer of shares, pre-emption rights

[50] The deed of foundation of the company may require the consent of the board of directors to any share transfer. Such consent may be withheld only for specific reasons listed in the deed of foundation or if the shares would be acquired by a competitor.

[51] In respect of a company limited by shares, other than in the case of a holder of preferential shares, there are no statutory pre-emption rights. However, shareholders may contractually agree with other shareholders or third persons on the establishment of pre-emption rights, or call or put options. All such transfer restrictions are effective vis-à-vis the company or a third person only if such rights have been indicated on the share certificate or registered in respect of the securities account.

5.2 Laws Affecting M&A

5.2.1 Laws and Regulations

[52] The legal framework governing transformations is set out in the Civil Code and the Transformations Act, which incorporates into Hungarian law the following European Directives:

(i) Directive (EU) 2019/2121 of the European Parliament and of the Council of 27 November 2019 amending Directive (EU) 2017/1132 as regards cross-border conversions, mergers and divisions.
(ii) 2017/1132/EU European Parliament and Council Directive relating to certain aspects of company law.
(iii) Sixth Council Directive 82/891/EEC on the division of public limited liability companies.
(iv) Directive 2005/56/EC on cross-border mergers of limited liability companies.
(v) Directive 2009/109/EC of the European Parliament and of the Council amending Council Directives 77/91/EEC, 78/855/EEC and 82/891/EEC, and Directive 2005/56/EC regarding reporting and documentation requirements in the case of mergers and divisions.
(vi) Directive 2011/35/EU of the European Parliament and of the Council concerning mergers of public limited liability companies.

In addition, the Cross-border Transformations Act also permits certain cross-border transformations.

[53] In addition to the above, the mergers and acquisitions of public companies are regulated by the Capital Market Act and, in some cases, sector-specific acts (acts regulating specific industry sectors, such as the Investment Service Providers Act and the Insurance Act). Given the diverse nature of the sector-specific legislation, we will not deal with it in this summary.

5.2.2 Most Common Transactions

[54] The following types of transformations are possible in Hungary:

(i) merger by acquisition (i.e., an existing company merging into another existing company, with the termination of the merging company);
(ii) merger by consolidation (fusion) (i.e., the formation of a new company from two or more companies);

(iii) cross-border mergers;
(iv) de-merger by spin-off (i.e., the formation of a new company, with the continuation of the original company); as of 01.01.2024 de-merger by spin-off may happen through detachment, where the original company will be the sole member of the new (detached) company;
(v) de-merger by separation (i.e., the formation of two new companies, with the termination of the original company); and
(vi) transformation of a company's legal form (cross-border transformations are now also implemented in Hungarian law).

[55] For takeovers and mandatory bids please *see* below in the passage dealing with Specific Rules on Public Takeovers.

Merger by acquisition

[56] In the event of a merger by acquisition, one or more companies are dissolved without liquidation and their business assets, including all rights and obligations, are transferred to the surviving company involved in the merger (the successor company). In principle, shareholders in the dissolving companies become shareholders in the successor company. Their shareholding in the successor company is determined by the proportion of the asset value of their shareholdings in the dissolving companies to the net asset value of the successor company.

Merger by consolidation (fusion)

[57] By contrast, in a merger by consolidation, two or more companies are dissolved without liquidation, and their business assets, including all rights and obligations, are transferred to a newly-established company. In principle, shareholders in the dissolving companies become shareholders in the newly-established company.

Cross-border transformations

[58] The Cross-border Transformation Act provides for the possibility of the cross-border merger of companies with different legal forms within the European Union, subject to the condition that the merger of companies with such legal forms is permitted by the local law of the countries of residence of such companies and (if applicable) by the country of residence of the successor company.

De-merger

[59] There are two forms of de-mergers under Hungarian law:

(i) de-merger by separation, where the assets and liabilities of the de-merged company are transferred to two or more newly-established companies and the predecessor company ceases to exist; or
(ii) de-merger by spin-off, where part of the assets and liabilities of the de-merged company remains with the de-merged company and part of the assets and liabilities is transferred to one or more newly-established successor companies. As of 1 January 2024, a company may carry out a de-merger by spin-off through 'detachment', where the original company will be the sole member of the newly established company.

[60] In the de-merger cases listed under paragraph (i) above, a company being split up ceases to exist without liquidation and its business assets, including all rights and obligations, are transferred to the successor companies. In principle, shareholders in the dissolving company become shareholders in the successor companies. Shareholders may become shareholders in either all of the successor companies or only in selected ones.

[61] In the de-merger cases listed under paragraph (ii) above, the de-merged entity survives the de-merger. The procedures for de-merger by spin-off are almost the same as 'classic' de-mergers, and the same legal regulations apply.

Transformation of a legal form

[62] Under Hungarian law, it is possible to change a company's current legal form to another without liquidation. The company with the new legal form remains the same legal entity as it was prior to the transformation (i.e., it is not dissolved), which has certain advantages – for example, any licences that do not depend on the legal form of the company remain in place. The transformation of the legal form of a company requires registration in the Companies' Register. The transformation procedure and requirements depend on the company type before and following the transformation.

5.2.3 Soft Law

[63] There are no 'soft law' sources such as voluntary codes, guidelines or self-regulation mechanisms in Hungary within the context of M&A transactions.

5.3 Relevant Regulatory Authorities

5.3.1 Corporate Filings

[64] The change in a company's ownership must be notified to the Court of Registration within thirty days of the effective date of such change. The Court of Registration registers the change of ownership within fifteen business days of the filing of all required documents.

5.3.2 Specific Authorities

[65] The acquisition of a 'qualified shareholding' or shares above certain thresholds is often conditional upon obtaining prior approval from the relevant regulatory authority, especially in the financial and energy sectors. The 'strictness' of the approval obligation, the thresholds, and the calculation of the thresholds (as well as the sanctions for failing to comply with the rules) vary sector by sector. It is recommended that investors wishing to invest in the finance, energy, media, and/or utility sectors carry out research in this respect before entering into binding agreements. (Note that often indirect shareholdings and changes of control are regulated.) It should also be noted that these approval obligations are separate from any obligations arising out of the public/private takeover or competition/antitrust regimes. Please find following a few examples of the involvement of authorities:

(i) In the case of the transfer of real estate, the change of ownership must be registered in the land registry.
(ii) A transaction may qualify as a concentration under Hungarian law; if the turnover thresholds are exceeded, then such transaction may be subject to merger clearance in Hungary.
(iii) Changes to the ownership of or licences to Intellectual Property (IP) registered in Hungary must be notified to the Hungarian Intellectual Property Office (HIPO) in writing. The registration of any change is likely to take thirty days.
(iv) For companies operating on regulated markets (such as the pharmaceuticals sector), additional notification obligations may apply (e.g., changes related to drug manufacturing requirements must be reported to the National Center for Public Health and Pharmacy, which decides within thirty days on the modification of the relevant drug manufacturing licence.

[66] If a legal entity conducts business in a regulated industry (e.g., the energy, banking, and insurance sectors, and in a number of other business sectors) without a licence or outside the scope of its licence, it may be subject to a fine (the range of sanctions varies industry-by-industry but almost always includes monetary fines).

5.4 Controls/ Restrictions on Foreign Investment

5.4.1 Restrictions on Acquisitions by Non-residents, Exchange Control

[67] In general, Hungarian law stipulates equal rights and obligations for both Hungarian and foreign legal entities (with some minor exceptions, such as laws relating to the purchase of agricultural land).

[68] Notwithstanding the above, since 1 January 2019 the transactions of foreign investors concerning specially regulated areas (e.g., banking and insurance), sensitive industrial sectors (e.g., gas/water/electricity supply, arms industry) and the communication system of Hungary, require prior notification/acknowledgement of the minister of the prime minister's cabinet office in accordance with Act LVII of 2018 on the monitoring of foreign investments detrimental to the interests of the national security of Hungary and the corresponding Governmental Decree 246/2018 (XII.17).

[69] In addition to the above, originally due to the COVID-19 pandemic, Hungary has introduced a new regime in Act LVIII of 2020 to screen foreign investments in order to protect Hungarian companies of strategic importance, i.e., the companies engaged in the activities listed in the Governmental Decree 289/2020 (VI.17), which runs parallel to the aforementioned procedure. Under such new regulations, the foreign investment falling under its scope has to be approved prior by the minister of economic development.

[70] Currently, there are no foreign exchange controls in place in Hungary.

5.4.2 Banking and Financial Services

[71] The establishment and operation of banks and other financial institutions are regulated by the Credit Institutions Act. Banks and credit institutions may only be established as companies limited by shares or through a branch office. Banks registered in a Member State may perform cross-border services on the territory of Hungary if so authorized in the Member State in which it is established (passporting regime). There is a minimum initial capital requirement, the level of which depends on the type of financial institution concerned. The initial capital of financial institutions must be paid in cash. To provide financial services, the authorization of the Hungarian National Bank (HNB) is required. Any person with a qualifying holding in a financial institution must be considered to be independent of any influences which may endanger the financial institution's sound, diligent and reliable operation, have a good business reputation and the capacity to provide reliable and diligent guidance and oversight of the financial institution and ensure transparency in business connections and ownership structure so as to allow the competent authority to exercise effective supervision over the financial institution.

5.4.3 Insurance

[72] The establishment and operation of insurance institutions are regulated by the Insurance Act. To provide insurance services the authorization of the HNB is required. Insurance companies may only be established as companies limited by shares, European companies limited by shares, cooperative societies, associations, or branch offices of foreign insurance companies or provide services on a cross-border basis (passporting). An insurance company, insurance intermediary or insurance consultant established in a Member State may perform cross-border services on the territory of Hungary or through its Hungarian branch if so authorized in the Member State in which it is established.

5.4.4 Membership of Foreigners of Executive Boards of Hungarian Companies and Business Travel Issues

[73] Hungarian law does not prohibit foreigners from taking executive positions in Hungarian companies. In fact, it does not even require that an employment contract be concluded between the parties for this purpose. Foreigners (just like Hungarian persons) may become, for example, managing directors of Hungarian companies on the basis of an employment contract or a mandate agreement.

[74] In respect of durations of stay, different provisions apply to:

(a) EU citizens, citizens of countries in the European Economic Area and citizens of countries with which Hungary has a bilateral agreement; and
(b) citizens of other (third) countries.

[75] The citizens of the countries referred to in point (a) may enter the territory of Hungary with a valid passport or identity card and may stay for a period of three months. A stay in excess of three months is only possible if the relevant citizen stays in Hungary for the purpose of occupational activities, or studies or has the financial means to cover such a stay. Subject to certain exceptions, the right of permanent residence will only be granted if the relevant citizen stays in Hungary continuously (without interruption) for five years. Only stays in excess of three months must be reported to the Office of Immigration and Nationality. In addition, if an employer wishes to employ such citizens, this must be reported to the competent labour authority.

[76] However, the citizens referred to in point (b) are required to apply for a visa to enter the territory of Hungary. In this respect, visas authorizing a stay of less than three months and visas for stays in excess of three months are distinguished. For occupational activities, a residency permit enabling a stay in Hungary of between three months and two years must be requested (this may be occasionally extended by two years). If an employer wishes to employ a citizen of a third country, the competent labour authority must be notified. A citizen of such a country may only perform work in Hungary on the basis of a work permit that has been issued by the labour authority.

5.4.5 Restriction on Acquiring Land

[77] Agricultural land may only be acquired (except for acquisition by inheritance) by Hungarian natural persons or citizens of the other Member States of the EU. Natural persons other than agricultural producers may not own more than one hectare of land. Undertakings and other entities may not acquire land (except for credit institutions issuing mortgages under special circumstances), neither by transfer of title nor by succession or merger – in the latter case the successor company will not acquire the land owned by its predecessor.

5.5 Incentives for Foreign Investment

5.5.1 Grants and Investment Incentives

[78] The legal basis for investment subsidies in Hungary is the common legal framework of the EU. The maximum regional subsidy intensity ratios are set by the European Commission periodically for each region. The ratio is adjusted for SMEs and large investment projects. Tax incentives are granted, *inter alia*, for investment projects with a net present value of at least HUF3 bn (approximately EUR7 96 m), investment projects above a certain value in certain sectors (e.g., R&D, movie industry), or investment projects above a certain value implemented by SMEs.

Investment incentives are available in cases regulated by Hungarian law. Any given incentives must be compatible with the internal market of the EU.

5.5.2 Tax Exemptions for Foreign Investment

[79] There are numerous investment tax incentives. Tax relief may be given on corporate tax and local industrial tax in cases regulated by the law. The investors may require provisional tax assessment related to a future transaction for the following five tax years, which can be prolonged by two years. The provisional tax assessment cannot be applied in case of a change in the relevant legislation or state of affairs.

Special economic zones

[80] The government has created benefits in the most underdeveloped areas, where additional state support is available for the investors. Moreover tax credits from corporate tax) are available, in some cases for several years, for investments above a certain value.

5.5.3 Guarantees Against Expropriation and Nationalization

[81] The constitution of Hungary declares that everybody has the right to property. Expropriation and nationalization are only permitted in exceptional cases, such as if such action is in the public interest. Hungarian law generally declares that the investments of foreigners enjoy full protection and security. The law guarantees that expropriation and nationalization may only be executed subject to full, unconditional and immediate compensation of the real value of the investment.

5.5.4 Repatriation of Profits

[82] The payments made by a company are regulated in the Civil Code:

(i) Payment to a member of the company including the payment of dividends abroad and the repatriation of profits is allowed except in the event that due to such payment, the company's equity would drop below its registered capital.

(ii) Dividends may be paid to a member entitled to exercise membership rights with respect to the company at the time of the decision on such payment of dividends.

5.5.5 Safeguards Concerning Foreign Loans in the Event of Liquidation

[83] There are no particular safeguards applicable to foreign loans specifically in the event of liquidation, i.e., they are treated in the same manner as domestic secured/ unsecured loans (as applicable).

5.5.6 Foreign Loans and Charges for IP Rights

[84] Contracts concerning foreign loans and charges to foreign companies for IP are regulated by the Civil Code. A choice of different law is possible.

5.5.7 Off-Shore Regulation

[85] It is permissible for local/domestic companies to hold offshore bank accounts. However, such bank accounts must appear in the Companies' Register.

5.5.8 Currency and Exchange Regulations

[86] In accordance with Act XCIII of 2001 on the Termination of Currency Restrictions and the Amendment of Certain Relating Legislation, no restriction on the transfer of currency shall apply, unless an act or decree states otherwise. At present, there are no foreign currency or foreign exchange controls in place. However, under extraordinary legal order situations, specific legislation could be implemented (e.g., by the president of Hungary or the Hungarian government) which could affect the possibility of transferring currency outside Hungary.

[87] For the sake of completeness, we note that there are EU-wide currency controls applicable to natural persons, e.g., any natural person entering or leaving the territory of the EU and carrying cash (or equivalent instruments such as cheques, travellers' cheques, promissory notes, money orders or gold) of a value of EUR10 000 or more shall declare that sum to the competent authorities of the given Member State.

6 SPECIFIC ISSUES OF COMPANY/SECURITIES LAW

6.1 Shareholder Approval

[88] In general, a merger must be approved on the basis of the authorization of the general meetings (or the sole members) of the participating companies. The transformation of a company must be approved by three-quarters of the votes represented at the general meeting. The approval right is exercised in the form of a resolution of the members' meeting or a sole member's written resolution. In the case of transfers of business shares, the other members, the company itself or a third party appointed by the members' meeting (in this order) have pre-emption rights.

6.2 Directors' Duties

[89] Directors have various duties in respect of M&A transactions, such as (i) the preparation of a proposal on change to the members of the company; (ii) the execution of corporate documents (e.g., a sale and purchase agreement, members list, declaration of acceptance); (iii) dealing with employee representation bodies; (iv) publishing information on a merger in the Companies Gazette; (v) cooperation with advisors, such as auditors.

[90] In the case of public takeovers, the management of a target company must refrain from frustrating the bid process. The board of directors is obliged to review the bid, issue its opinion on it and publish this opinion. Also, the board of directors must appoint an independent financial expert, whose opinion must also be published. Moreover, it is the board's obligation to forward the bid to the representatives of the employees so that they may also issue an opinion.

6.3 Form of Consideration

[91] According to the Civil Code cash and non-cash consideration is permitted in the following forms: (i) ownership rights; (ii) tangible or intangible assets; and (iii) a receivable (if it is acknowledged by the debtor or if it is based on a final court ruling).

6.4 Restrictions

[92] The amount of a cash contribution at the time of the foundation of private companies limited by shares may not be less than 30% of the share capital.

6.5 Valuation Process

[93] A formal valuation process is only required if the non-cash consideration is provided to private companies limited by shares. Certain exceptions to this rule are stipulated by law.

6.6 Financial Assistance

[94] Under Hungarian law, limited liability companies and private companies limited by shares are not prohibited from providing financial assistance for the purchase of their own shares.

[95] Restrictions only apply to public companies limited by shares. Public companies limited by shares may only give financial assistance under market conditions and from the assets available for the payment of dividends, provided that the general meeting approves such a decision by at least a three-quarter majority upon the recommendation of the board of directors of the company. The recommendation must contain the reasons for such financial assistance, the risks involved, the conditions, the price of the shares and the advantages the company is likely to gain by providing such financial assistance. The recommendation must be submitted to the court of registry. The applicable laws do not stipulate any exemptions from these provisions and there are no 'whitewash' procedures.

[96] With regard to the consequences, any financial assistance (loan, security, guarantee, etc.) granted by a public company limited by shares in breach of this restriction will be void.

6.7 Security Interests

Types of Security Interest

[97] In acquisition financing, the lenders usually require a full security package securing the bank loan from each of the special purpose vehicles (if any), the target and those of the target's subsidiaries that are located in Hungary in order to secure the acquisition facility. Such security package usually consists of the following security interests over the company's assets:

(i) mortgage over real estate;
(ii) pledge over quotas/shares or security deposit over shares of companies;
(iii) charge over movable assets;
(iv) pledge over rights (including IP rights) and receivables (including trade receivables and intercompany receivables);
(v) pledge or security deposit over bank accounts;
(vi) security deposit over cash;
(vii) prohibition of alienation and encumbrance over real estates (simultaneously with mortgage and/or call option);
(viii) in some cases, call option established for security purposes over real estate and quotas/shares of companies is usually used simultaneously with pledges/mortgages established over the same asset; and
(ix) in some cases, security assignment of receivables is usually used simultaneously with receivables pledges.

[98] In addition to the above in rem security interests, Hungarian companies may undertake a suretyship/guarantee guaranteeing the obligations of an intra-group borrower under the acquisition bank loan.

6.8 Security Interest Similar to Floating Charge

[99] Currently, there is no dedicated floating charge under the Hungarian regime regulating collateral. However, the Civil Code stipulates that a pledge may be created over the scope of assets owned by the pledgor, as described in the underlying security agreement. Therefore, a Hungarian company may grant a pledge over all non-registered assets, rights and receivables owned by the Hungarian company from time to time. Such security works in essence as a floating charge over such assets.

6.9 Registration and Perfection of Security Interests

[100] In order to create a valid and fully perfected pledge over assets, a pledge is registered in the following public registers:

(i) mortgage (pledge) over real estate in the land registry;
(ii) pledge over registered movable assets in their specific register;
(iii) pledge over copyrights in the copyright register;
(iv) pledge over patents in the patent register; and
(v) pledge over non-registered movable assets, rights and receivables, bank accounts and floating-type charges in the security interests register.

[101] In order to create a valid and fully perfected pledge over the above assets, the pledgor must have a right of disposal over the relevant asset, either by way of transferring the possession of such asset to the security beneficiary (in respect of possessory pledges over movable assets, where no dedicated registry is available) or by registering the pledge into the relevant public registry referred to above. If the pledgor is not registered in the relevant registry, the pledgee can only enforce its rights under the pledge agreement *vis-á-vis* the pledgor but it cannot enforce those rights vis-á-vis third parties.

[102] Security deposits and possessory pledges over movable assets are not required to be registered in public registers. Such security interests are perfected by handing over the relevant assets over which the security interest is created to the depositee/pledgee or in case of security deposit over bank accounts or shares, by blocking the respective bank or securities account.

6.10 Enforcement of Security Interests Outside Liquidation/Bankruptcy

[103] Once a secured obligation becomes due and the debtor has defaulted, the pledge can be enforced through court enforcement proceedings or through different out-of-court proceedings (except in the case of a pledge over bank accounts, which is only enforceable through court enforcement proceedings). Possibilities for out-of-court enforcement include the sale of a pledged asset, the acquisition of a pledged asset and the enforcement of a pledged claim or right. The pledgee is free to choose from the available enforcement methods.

[104] Depending on the form of the suretyship/guarantee agreement, a suretyship/guarantee may be executed through court proceedings or notary proceedings.

6.11 Enforcement of Security Interests in Bankruptcy

[105] In the case of bankruptcy proceedings, the debtor is being granted a moratorium. The general moratorium expires at the beginning of the second business day following the 180th day after the commencement date of the bankruptcy proceedings. However, the court, upon request of the debtor, may extend the duration of the general moratorium for up to a maximum of 240 and/or 365 calendar days, provided that the request of the debtor is supported by a certain majority of creditors.

[106] During the moratorium, the security holders cannot enforce their security interests established by the debtor save for certain exceptions (e.g., security deposit for a certain period of time).

6.12 Enforcement of Security Interests in Liquidation

[107] Claims secured by a pledge/mortgage and registered within the applicable forty days deadline enjoy priority over the mandatory order of payment (as set out by law). After the deduction of certain costs (e.g., taxes and administrative service fees and costs of maintenance of records and the fees of the liquidator (up to a specified threshold)), all sales proceeds of pledged assets are exclusively used for the satisfaction of claims secured by the pledge/mortgage. Claims that remain outstanding following the application of the above rules fall under the mandatory order of payment.

[108] In addition, claims secured by security deposits over certain assets (e.g., cash or bank accounts) could be satisfied directly before these claims for a limited period of time.

[109] According to the Bankruptcy Act, creditors with a security deposit (which was established prior to the commencement date of the liquidation proceedings) over certain assets (e.g., cash or bank accounts) are allowed to directly enforce their claims within three months from the commencement date of the liquidation proceedings.

6.13 Claw-Back Risks in Bankruptcy Proceedings

[110] Asset inspectors may challenge contracts of the debtor that were entered into without the asset inspector's approval or countersignature, or reclaim payments that were made in breach of the general prohibition on payments during the moratorium. The legal consequence of a successful challenge is the invalidity of the underlying contracts or payments.

6.14 Claw-Back Risks in Liquidation Proceedings

[111] The legislation entitles creditors and liquidators to challenge certain contracts of the debtor. Importantly, besides meeting the formal conditions below, claimants must invoke a provision of substantive law (such as the fraudulent nature of the contract) in order to be successful in court.

[112] Within one year after the commencement date of the liquidation proceedings, creditors and liquidators may challenge contracts entered into by the debtor which:

(i) have resulted in the reduction of the debtor's assets and have been entered into within five years before the submission date of the liquidation request, provided that the debtor's intention was to jeopardize the interests of creditors and the other party knew or should have known about the debtor's intention (*fraudulent transactions*);

(ii) aim the transfer of the assets of the debtor without consideration, the assumption of obligations regarding the debtor's assets without consideration or the granting of a significant benefit to a third party at a significantly disproportionate discount price, provided that such contracts have been entered into within three years before the submission date of the liquidation request (*undervalued transactions*);

(iii) give a preference to a particular creditor, provided that it was entered into within ninety days before the submission date of the liquidation request (*preferential transactions*); and

(iv) have been concluded within three years before the submission date of the liquidation request or thereafter, or his other commitments, if made for the purpose of transfer of ownership by way of guarantee, or the assignment of a right or claim by way of a guarantee or exercising a collateralized option to buy, where the beneficiary exercised such acquired right by failing to fulfil his obligation of accounting toward the debtor or did so improperly, and/or failed to pay the amount remaining after the secured claim is satisfied; if the right-holder did not have the acquisition of ownership, or the assignment of a right or claim by way of a guarantee registered in the collateral register, or his buy option in the real estate register, the conditions for lodging a contest shall be presumed to exist.

[113] The legal consequence of a successful challenge is the invalidity of the underlying contracts. In connection with fraudulent and undervalued transactions, the bad faith of the parties and the lack of consideration are assumed by law if the particular contracts were entered into between the debtor and certain of its connected persons (broadly shareholders, executives, related entities).

[114] The liquidators may also reclaim performed contractual obligations or terminate any contracts of the debtor save for certain limited exceptions. In the context of reclaim, any service can be reclaimed (within deadlines applicable for the challenge of contracts) that was performed by the debtor within sixty days before the date on which the request for liquidation proceedings is received by the court if such service did not fall within the scope of the debtor's ordinary course of business and granted an unjustifiable preference to a particular creditor.

6.15 Completion Formalities

[115] A change in a company's ownership must be notified to the Court of Registration within thirty days of the effective date of the acquisition. The Court of Registration registers the change in ownership within fifteen business days of the filing of all required documents.

[116] It is important to note that the title to the shares transfers on the date of the parties' agreement and not when the court of registration registers the change in ownership.

[117] Receivables may be taken over by way of an assignment of rights and obligations or may be transferred by way of an assumption of debts. Contracts can be also transferred by way of a contract transfer regulated in the Civil Code. Counterparty approval is required in all cases.

[118] For assets other than real estate, no notarization or other formalities apply. For the transfer of real estate, the transfer agreement must be in Hungarian, notarized or countersigned by a Hungarian lawyer or be in the form of a notarial deed, and its content must be compliant with the Hungarian statutory requirements.

Transformations

[119] There are various formalities to be fulfilled, which depend on the type of merging companies and the structure in question. For instance, mergers of entities with the same sole shareholder are more straightforward in practice than mergers of entities with a number of different shareholders.

[120] The merger process involves, in particular, the following key steps:

(a) determination of the merger date;
(b) preparation of the relevant financial statements (in a number of cases, these need to be audited);
(c) preparation and execution of the merger plan;
(d) preparation and execution of the merger agreement;

(e) preparation of other merger documents by the statutory bodies;
(f) publication of certain information relating to the merger in the Companies' Register;
(g) approval of the merger by the general meetings of the companies involved;
(h) registration of the merger in the Companies' Register; and
(i) exchange of shares and payments of compensation, if applicable.

6.16 Costs and Fees

[121] Negligible stamp duty is payable on the transfer of shares when the corporate documents are filed with the court of registration.

[122] Transfer taxes are payable if the following assets are transferred: (i) real estate; (ii) qualifying real estate holding company interests (e.g., shares); (iii) rights with monetary value adjacent to real estate (e.g., usufruct); or (iv) certain vehicles (e.g., cars).

6.17 Dividends

[123] Dividends may be paid to the members of a company registered in the shareholders' list at the time of the decision on the payment of the dividends.

[124] The after-tax profit for the year and the retained earnings used to supplement the after-tax profit may be disbursed as a dividend only if the amount of equity less the tied-up reserves and the valuation reserve, does not fall below the amount of the registered capital of the company following the disbursement of the dividend.

6.18 Purchase of Own Shares

[125] There are certain restrictions on a company's ability to redeem or purchase its own shares. A limited liability company may purchase its own business shares from those that exceed the equity. The company may not acquire its own business shares if it is not authorized to pay dividends. Private companies limited by shares are entitled to acquire their own shares up to 25% of the share capital. Private companies limited by shares are not entitled to subscribe for shares of their own issue during the process of foundation or when increasing the share capital.

6.19 The Corporate Veil

[126] If a company is terminated without legal succession, claims that remain unsatisfied can be enforced within five years of the de-registration of the company against those shareholders that were shareholders in the company at the time that it was de-registered from the Companies' Register. As a general rule, the members of a company that is dissolved without a legal successor have only limited liability vis-à-vis third persons; they will be held liable for the outstanding debts of the dissolved company only to the extent of their respective shares in distributed company assets.

[127] However, any shareholder who has abused its limited liability may not rely on its limited liability. The Civil Code is silent about possible cases involving abuse of limited liability. Nevertheless, the examples referred to by previous regulation (before the entry into force of the Civil Code) should apply to other possible scenarios. Shareholders are liable if, for example, the shareholders have disposed of assets of the company as if they were their own, or if they have reduced the assets of the company for the benefit of others or themselves when they knew (or should have known) that the company would not be able to satisfy its obligations towards third parties as a result of such conduct.

6.20 Permanently Adverse Business Policy

[128] While as a general rule, the shareholders of a company have limited liability towards third persons in respect of any obligations of the company towards creditors that are not covered by its assets, unlimited liability might be established by the court at the request of any creditor during or at the end of the liquidation proceedings on the basis of conducting permanently adverse business policy. The court may theoretically establish a shareholder's unlimited liability only if: (i) it can be proven that it directly or indirectly disposes of at least 75% of the votes in the company; (ii) the controlling shareholder was conducting a 'permanently adverse business policy' in respect of the company; (iii) liquidation proceedings are commenced against the company; (iv) there is a causal link between the 'permanently adverse business policy' and the insolvency of the company; and (v) the assets of the company do not cover all the claims of its creditors.

6.21 'Shadow Director Concept'

[129] Hungarian law acknowledges the 'shadow director' concept, which might be a basis for establishing the liability of a shareholder. Under the regime governing 'wrongful trading', the directors of a company must act in the interests of creditors once they foresee or should have been able to foresee that the company may become insolvent (i.e., the company is in a 'threat of insolvency' situation). A threat of insolvency arises at the date on which the directors of a company foresee or could have reasonably foreseen that the company will not be able to satisfy its debts when they are due. The shadow director concept is a rather broad concept on the basis of which liability may also be established in respect of a person who, while not being formally a director of the debtor, had in fact 'decisively influenced' the decisions of the debtor.

6.22 Insolvency

[130] In liquidation proceedings, if the company's debts exceed 50% of its registered capital, the court, upon the filing of a petition by a creditor, could establish that the former majority owner who transferred his/her holding in such company within three years prior to the commencement of the liquidation proceedings is subject to unlimited liability for the company's outstanding debt.

[131] The majority owner could be exempted from unlimited liability only if the majority owner is able to prove that:

(i) the company was solvent at the time of transfer and that the threat of insolvency/insolvency occurred subsequently; or
(ii) although the company was insolvent/in threat of insolvency, the majority owner has acted in good faith taking into account the interests of creditors while transferring its shareholding.

[132] In the case of dissolution without a legal successor to the company, a former member is liable for the company's debts but only to the extent the former member received assets from the liquidated company following its termination without a legal successor.

6.23 General Background of Hungarian Insolvency Law

[133] The following two basic types of insolvency proceedings are regulated by the Bankruptcy Act. Both proceedings are ordered and administered by the court:

(i) Bankruptcy proceedings, whereby a debtor, in order to reach a bankruptcy settlement agreement with its creditors, is granted a payment moratorium without winding up (terminating) the debtor. Bankruptcy proceedings may be initiated by the debtor, but the insolvency of the debtor is not a prerequisite for filing for bankruptcy proceedings. During the moratorium, debtors are operating their businesses but are subject to several restrictions including the supervision of their affairs by court-appointed asset inspectors, and creditors are restricted to exercise or enforce their rights under their finance agreements. The bankruptcy settlement agreement is a written contract whereby a debtor and its creditors agree on any measures deemed to be necessary for the successful turnaround of the debtor. Bankruptcy settlement agreements typically set out a plan of reorganization including provisions on debt re-scheduling or restructuring. Bankruptcy proceedings are relatively short in practice, because the duration of the moratorium may not exceed 365 days under any circumstances.

(ii) Liquidation proceedings, which aim to secure the satisfaction of creditors' claims in the course of winding up the insolvent debtor without a legal successor. While no moratorium is granted to debtors, as a general rule the creditors may not directly enforce their claims because court-appointed liquidators are authorized to enforce all claims by selling the assets of the debtor. Liquidation proceedings may also be initiated by both debtors and creditors, but the insolvency of the debtor is a prerequisite for filing. The legislation sets out circumstances when the court must declare the insolvency of the debtor. The most typical of these is a situation when the debtor is unable to meet its payment obligations within twenty days of such obligations becoming due, provided the debtor has not disputed its payment obligation prior. At the commencement date of the liquidation proceedings (which is generally the date of publication of the court decree ordering the commencement of the proceedings) shareholders and executives statutorily lose their rights and entitlements regarding debtors, and the proceedings (and largely the affairs of debtors) are managed by the liquidators. Liquidation proceedings may last for several (two, three or even more) years in practice.

6.24 Choice of Law

[134] In many transactions, in particular transactions with a significant foreign element, Hungarian law allows parties to agree that the relevant contract may be governed by a law other than Hungarian law. However, the transaction transfer remains subject to mandatory Hungarian legal requirements. In the case of national assets, the choice of foreign law is invalid.

7 SPECIFIC RULES ON PUBLIC TAKEOVERS

[135] Public takeovers in Hungary are regulated by the Capital Market Act, which implements a number of capital markets-related directives of the EU, including the 2017/1132/EU European Parliament and Council Directive, the so-called Takeover Directive. Other related rules that may be applicable to public takeovers if the Capital Market Act does not provide specific rules on certain issues are set out in the Civil Code. Last but not least, the listing rules of the Budapest Stock Exchange also contain relevant rules relating to public takeover bids. The general supervisory authority having competence in connection with public takeovers is the HNB.

7.1 General Principles

[136] The public takeover rules are applicable to public companies limited by shares where the shares of the given company are either listed on the Budapest Stock Exchange or where the shares of a public company have been issued in Hungary but are not listed on any regulated markets.

[137] In principle, three types of public takeovers may be differentiated under Hungarian law:

(a) mandatory takeovers (i.e., where a shareholder has already passed certain thresholds of share ownership (representing voting rights) and must make a bid for the rest of the company's shares);
(b) voluntary takeovers; and
(c) squeeze-out or put option right of minority shareholders following a successful bid in a public company.

7.2 Mandatory Takeover Bid

[138] It is mandatory to launch a public takeover bid procedure in advance of the proposed acquisition of voting shares in a target company if, as a result of the acquisition, the acquirer intends to acquire voting rights of: (i) more than 25% in the target company provided that there is no other person that holds at least 10% of the voting rights in the target company; or (ii) more than 33% provided that there is at least one other person that holds at least a 10% of the voting rights in the target company.

[139] Stakebuilding is possible as long as the thresholds of the mandatory takeover bid rules are not reached but after reaching such thresholds it is mandatory to prepare a takeover bid. If the bidder crosses the 25% or 33% threshold (as the case may be) as a result of the bid, the bidder does not have to launch a new bid in the future if it intends to purchase further shares (acquire further influence) in the target company.

7.3 Voluntary Takeover Bid

[140] A party may launch a voluntary takeover bid even if it was not mandatory (e.g., the investor would not cross the relevant thresholds or the investor already made a public offer and crossed the threshold). In principle, in a voluntary takeover bid, the rules of the mandatory takeover bid are applicable except that in the case of a voluntary bid, the amended offer terms as to the price of the shares may be less than the initial offer price, the board of directors of the target company is not obliged to issue an opinion on the bid or mandate an independent financial expert for the review of the bid and there may be no counter-takeover bid made.

7.4 Squeeze-Out

[141] A squeeze-out of the minority shareholders of a target company may be executed after a successful public takeover only if the bidder has reserved this right in the bid documentation. In such event, the bidder may purchase the shares of minority shareholders within three months from the end of the acceptance period of the initial public takeover procedure, provided that the bidder acquired at least 90% of the shares (voting rights) in the target company prior to exercising this right.

[142] Nevertheless, it should also be noted that if the bidder ends up with at least 90% of the shares (voting rights) in the target company as a result of the bid, the minority shareholders may sell their stakes to the bidder within three months from the date on which the target company published the acquisition of the shares (voting rights).

7.5 Takeover Bid Procedure

7.5.1 Due Diligence Procedure

[143] There is no explicit regulation or constraint regarding legal due diligence in a takeover procedure. In principle, investors may rely on the following two main publicly available information sources:

(i) the official public registries holding certain data of companies with their registered seats in Hungary such as, among others, the following:
  (a) articles and company extracts setting out directors, registered capital, supervisory board members, auditors, registered seat and other corporate data;
  (b) audited annual reports;
  (c) IP rights registered with the Hungarian patent office;
  (d) real property owned by the target company; and
  (e) registered charges e.g., floating charges, liens, etc.).

(ii) for listed securities, the publications of the target company are made on the website of the Budapest Stock Exchange (e.g., quarterly reports, extraordinary publications, etc.).

7.5.2 Approval and Notification Requirements

HNB approval

[144] The bidder together with an investment firm, which the bidder is required to appoint to manage the bidding process, must submit the bid to the HNB for approval prior to the intended takeover (acquisition) and, simultaneously, the same bid must also be sent to the board of directors of the target company for information purposes. The bid and the formal request addressed to the HNB for approval

of the bid are required to contain the information and documents described and detailed in the Capital Market Act. The HNB must not refuse the granting of the approval to the bid if the bid document complies with the requirements of the Capital Market Act.

[145] The general deadline for the HNB to issue its approval on the bid is ten business days starting on the date when the takeover bid is submitted to it for approval. The HNB may request further documents, attachments or details by setting a deadline to submit the additional information within three business days and the HNB has three business days to resolve the approval of the bid after the receipt of all additional documents. If the HNB does not issue any resolution by the above deadlines, the approval is deemed to be granted.

7.5.3 Bid Duration

[146] The period during which shareholders are able to sell their shares to the bidder, i.e., to accept the bid by issuing an acceptance declaration, may not be less than thirty calendar days, and may not be more (including any extension of the deadline) than sixty-five calendar days (so-called acceptance period). The starting date of the acceptance period must be a date between the second and the fifth day after the date of the publication of the HNB approval of the bid. The HNB may, pursuant to the reasonable request of the bidder, consent to an extension of the acceptance period, which extension may not be more than fifteen calendar days.

7.5.4 Takeover Bid Price and Collateral

[147] The Capital Market Act provides for a long list of complex calculation methods of the bid price. In principle, in the case of listed shares, the minimum bid price for the shares must be at least the highest of the following:

(i) the volume-weighted average market price of the respective shares during a 180-day period ending on the date of the submission of the bid to the HNB for approval; or
(ii) the highest price agreed by the bidder or an affiliate of the bidder for the target company's shares during a 180-day period ending on the date of the submission of the bid to the HNB for approval; or
(iii) if available, the volume-weighted average stock market price of the target company's shares during a 360-day period ending on the date of the submission of the bid to the HNB for approval; or
(iv) the aggregate of the agreed call price and the commission fee paid for the target company's shares in connection with a call option or a repurchase option exercised by the bidder or an affiliate of the bidder during a 180-day period ending on the date of the submission of the bid to the HNB for approval; or
(v) the aggregate of the agreed call price and the commission fee agreed in an agreement for the target company's shares, during a 180-day period ending

on the date of the submission of the bid to the HNB for approval, in connection with a call option or a repurchase option to be exercised by the bidder or an affiliate of the bidder; or

(vi) the consideration received for exercising voting rights by the bidder or an affiliate of the bidder in the target company on the basis of an agreement concluded for the purposes of acting in concert, during a 180-day period ending on the date of the submission of the bid to the HNB for approval; or

(vii) the value of equity per share in the target company.

[148] In connection with the consideration, the bid must contain evidence that the bidder has the necessary financial means to provide the consideration for the shares in the target company. The HNB only accepts the following as sufficient evidence for the payment of such consideration:

(i) cash;
(ii) debt security issued by an EU or OECD Member State; or
(iii) a bank guarantee issued by a bank with a registered seat in an EU or OECD Member State.

[149] In a public takeover procedure, it is not possible to make a partial offer only for a certain portion of the shares to which voting rights are attached and the terms offered to the shareholders must be the same for each of the shareholders, i.e., no discrimination is allowed in the bid. Although the practice is that cash is offered as consideration for the shares in public takeovers, it is also possible to offer securities as consideration for the shares.

7.6 Conditional Bid

[150] There is only one condition that is expressly mentioned under the Capital Market Act that may be established as the basis for withdrawing from the bid. Such a condition is that withdrawal is possible only if the voting rights that would be acquired in the target company as a result of the acceptance declarations would not represent more than 50% of all voting rights. Please note that it is yet untested whether any other condition could be validly stipulated in the bid, such as the raising of adequate financing or a 'material adverse change' clause. The better interpretation should be that other conditions may also be stipulated in the bid. However, any other condition (other than the withdrawal condition referred to above) would be evaluated by the HNB in a so-called all facts and circumstances test.

7.6.1 Counter-Takeover Bid

[151] A counter-takeover bid can only be launched after an initial takeover bid has been launched and approved by the HNB but not later than the fifteenth day preceding the last day of the acceptance period of the initial takeover bid. A counter-takeover bid is only valid if the consideration for the shares in the target company is at least 5% higher in HUF than the previous bid price. If the counter-takeover bid differs from a previous bid only in respect of the amount of consideration, the HNB will decide on the approval within three days. When the approved counter-bid is published, the previous bid (and the acceptances) become ineffective. In all other respects, the provisions applicable to the counter-takeover bid are equally applicable to a 'general' takeover bid.

7.6.2 Discretion Rules

[152] If before the publication of the takeover bid the management body of the target company upon the bidder's request has provided any information to the bidder or his proxy concerning the operations of the company, the bidder, his proxy, and the investment service provider commissioned shall handle such information as strictly confidential in compliance with the regulations on business secrets, securities secrets and insider dealing. In case of breach of confidentiality, the legal consequences must be settled by agreement between the parties. In the absence of such an agreement, the chosen tort law will be applicable.

7.7 Takeover Bid Related Issues

7.7.1 Prohibition on Trading in Shares

[153] Until the expiry of the period within which shareholders of the target company may accept the bid by issuing their declaration of acceptance, the bidder and any person acting in concert with the bidder, or who is an affiliate of the bidder, are prohibited from selling, purchasing or agreeing to sell or purchase or otherwise transfer the target company's shares in any manner other than through the takeover bid. It is important to note that this prohibition applies from the date of submission of the bid documentation to the HNB for approval until the acceptance period is open. In addition, the investment firm managing the bid is also prohibited from entering into own-account transactions with respect to the shares (except that the investment firm may sell its own shares to the bidder within the scope of the bid process).

7.7.2 Target Company's Obligations

[154] Although this is not a possibility that is often used, the articles of the target company may provide that from the moment of the publication of the notification of takeover intent until the completion of the takeover bid process, the target company's board of directors may not act to frustrate the bid process. However, even if the articles contain such a prohibition, the board of directors of the target company may still act to encourage a counter-bid, and take all actions that have been authorized by the general meeting prior to the launch of the bid (provided that such action is within the normal course of business).

[155] The board of directors is obliged to review the bid and issue its opinion on it. Such an opinion of the board of directors must be published before the acceptance period opens. In principle, the board of directors must also appoint an independent financial expert, whose opinion must also be published and be consistent with its own opinion. Furthermore, the board of directors is also required to forward the bid to the representatives of the employees so that they may also issue an opinion in which event this has to form part of the opinion of the board of directors.

7.7.3 Non-compliance with Applicable Takeover Rules

[156] In the event an investor acquires voting rights in breach of any of the public takeover rules set out in the Capital Market Act, such an investor cannot exercise its voting rights in the target company.

[157] The investor must dispose of the shares (voting rights), acquired as a result of the breach, within sixty days of the acquisition or the resolution of the HNB determining the breach and the investor cannot exercise any shareholder rights in the target company for as long as the shares (voting rights) acquired in breach of the mandatory rules are not disposed of.

[158] In addition to the above, the HNB may impose a penalty on an investor breaching the rules on public takeovers. In principle, the amount of the penalty which may be imposed on the investor for a breach of the mandatory rules may be a maximum of HUF2 bn (approximately EUR5.30 m) in a worst-case scenario, but the actual amount is determined within the HNB's discretion based on the individual circumstances.

8 OTHER RELEVANT LAWS AND DUE DILIGENCE ISSUES

8.1 Anti-bribery and Anti-corruption Laws

[159] The criminal legal framework on corruption covers both the private and the public sectors. This framework provides for an adequate level of protection according to the Council of Europe Group of States against Corruption (GRECO). The EU Framework Decision 2003/568/JHA on combating corruption in the private sector has been transposed and the provisions of Directive 2019/1937 on the protection of persons who report breaches of Union law have been also implemented in a new legislation.

[160] In spite of the recent improvements, the risk of corruption most notably in the area of public procurement persists, the effectiveness of control mechanisms throughout the procurement cycle and the post-award phase are still facing challenges, particularly at the local level.

8.2 Money-Laundering Regulations

[161] Hungary has fully implemented the anti-money laundering and anti-terrorist financing framework of the EU.

8.3 Registration and Enforcement of IP Rights

[162] IP rights are registered with the HIPO. The legal provisions applicable for the registration proceedings and the granting of IP protection are set out at the EU level. The conduct of the HIPO reflects the common practice of the relevant authorities of the Member States. The electronically accessible register can be inspected at any time free of charge and authentic certificates can also be requested.

[163] Moreover, Hungary is a member of the European Patent Convention, the Paris Convention for the Protection of Industrial Property, the Berne Convention for the Protection of Literary and Artistic Works, the WIPO Copyright Treaty and other important treaties on international protection of IP rights.

8.4 Indemnities to Agents or Distributors on Termination

[164] European Union Directive 86/653/EEC on self-employed commercial agents was transposed to Hungarian law. Accordingly, agents are entitled to commission on transactions they have procured for their principal even if the transaction is concluded after the termination of the agency contract; and they can also be entitled to reasonable indemnification (maximum the average annual remuneration) if certain conditions continue to apply.

8.5 The Due Diligence Process

8.5.1 Introduction

[165] Purchasers normally carry out an investigation into the legal, financial, technological and environmental position of a target company, as well as all relevant and related circumstances. Therefore, sellers are also familiar with this process. Legal due diligence is conducted once the seller has committed to sell the target and the purchaser has expressed a strong interest in acquiring the target, often by signing either a 'letter of intent' or a 'memorandum of understanding'. At this stage, all relevant legal relationships, the validity of existing agreements and other legal matters need to be clarified so that a final decision in respect of the acquisition can be taken. The scope of the due diligence investigation depends on the purchaser's requirements. In most cases, a full legal due diligence is carried out, i.e., the commercial, financial, tax, environmental, etc., issues are dealt with. Nevertheless, it also depends on the sector in which the target company operates, which fields are considered to be material in the context of the transaction and therefore which areas are inspected by the purchaser. For example, in the case of a manufacturing target company, environmental issues are likely to be material, whereas in the case of a target company merely engaged in commercial activities such issues are normally not investigated.

8.5.2 Title Investigation and Environmental Audits

[166] The investigation of title depends on whether the property in question is real property or movable assets. In the case of real property, typically the data contained in the real estate register is investigated as the registration itself creates the title over real property. A couple of years ago it was also typical to conduct a chain of title investigation, but this is no longer customary, as the real estate register validly evidences the ownership of a property until proven otherwise. Title investigation in relation to movable assets is normally only done in respect of special types of movable assets of great value which are registered in special registries, such as vehicles, ships or aircraft.

[167] Environmental audits are only carried out in the case of target companies whose operations may give rise to environmental issues.

8.5.3 Data Rooms

[168] Nowadays usually a virtual data room is set up for the purposes of the review of the documents in transactions, however, in less frequent cases a physical data room or the handover of printed documents is used.

8.5.4 Special Investigations

[169] In the case of companies operating in regulated markets, such as banks, energy sector operators or pharmaceutical companies, the holding of specific licences or permits is of crucial importance. During the course of the due diligence investigation of such target companies, it is investigated whether the target company holds all necessary licences and permits and whether those can be transferred.

8.5.5 Quality of Data Rooms

[170] In respect of data rooms, it is typical that sellers undertake to provide a full data room based on a due diligence request list received from the purchaser's advisers. It often turns out that when the purchaser's advisers start the due diligence process the great majority of the documents to be reviewed have not been provided by the sellers, which may result in significant delays in the process.

[171] In the case of a particularly well-handled data room, the sellers make available the documents listed by the purchaser's advisors in a timely manner and upload such documents in a clearly organized virtual data room.

8.5.6 Representations, Warranties and Indemnities

[172] If specific issues cannot be investigated based on the data room, representations and warranties are typically inserted into the SPA, in which the seller represents that certain facts are true and correct and undertakes a warranty obligation based on which it shall be liable if they prove to be inaccurate. Indemnities are also used in the case of issues that are discovered from information contained in the data room and the seller undertakes to indemnify the purchaser for damage arising from such issues or circumstances. These methods are commonly used in Hungary in the context of M&A transactions.

[173] According to our experience, in the case of a breach of representations, warranties and indemnities, the issues are typically resolved amicably between the parties and resort to litigation is very rare.

8.5.7 Role of Courts and Other Relevant Dispute Resolution Mechanisms

[174] There are several types of dispute resolution mechanisms available in Hungary. The most common ones are the ordinary courts, arbitration courts (both general and sector-specific) and assorted mediation methods.

[175] The ordinary court system provides for two-instance dispute settlement, with the additional possibility of a supervision procedure by the Supreme Court. Generally, regular court proceedings are lengthy and open to the public, therefore in business disputes, alternative dispute resolution methods are preferred. Arbitration is commonly chosen for faster dispute settlement and discretion, in spite of the significant costs that arise in association with it. Arbitration decisions are recognized and enforced the same way as the judgments of the regular courts, compliant with the relevant international standards. Arbitration decisions are not subject to appeal, but their annulment can be requested on very limited grounds.

[176] Settlements concluded in the course of mediation may be filed with the court in order to make them legally binding and enforceable.

8.5.8 Preference for Consumers over Businesses

[177] For consumer protection reasons, the courts are in certain cases required by law to favour consumers over businesses, but such requirements are in line with European Union legislation on consumer protection. Generally, no preference is given to domestic residents or companies over foreigners.

8.5.9 Independence and Competence of the Judiciary

[178] The independence of courts is protected at the highest level of law (in the Constitution), in various statutes and by financial and organizational separation from the government and government agencies. Nonetheless, on the one hand, the independence of the courts has been called into question from time to time, especially when the courts have decided cases involving major social or political issues, but overall the courts are still considered to reject political influence. The independence of judges, on the other hand, results in somewhat different levels of competence at the various courts, particularly in the countryside, whereas the more complex cases before the Metropolitan Court are typically handled professionally.

[179] Despite various efforts and legislative changes intended to speed up court procedures, it takes more time in general to get a case heard in the ordinary courts as compared to the arbitration courts. However, a lot of progress has been made in the last years under the new codes of procedures, which shortened the average length of procedures by years. A final and binding judgment (including the appeal procedure before the second instance court) can be reached in a simple matter within one or two years if it is conducted in a smaller city court with no substantial backlog of cases. In matters with a more complex fact pattern and involving Metropolitan courts and/or an expert opinion, a final and binding judgment can take several years.

8.5.10 Enforceability of Key Contractual Provisions

[180] Key contractual provisions in line with Hungarian law can generally be enforced at the court. A contractual provision is not enforceable if it is deemed invalid by law. The grounds for invalidity are regulated in detail in the Civil Code.

9 MERGER CONTROLS: ANTITRUST/ COMPETITION ISSUES

9.1 Relevant Legislation and Competent Authorities

[181] The main law regulating merger control in Hungary is the Competition Act, which has been amended several times since it came into effect on 1 January 1997. Laws regulating sectors such as pharmaceutical supplies and the media set out further specific rules on the permissibility of concentrations in these sectors.

[182] The main authority involved is the Hungarian Competition Authority ('HCA'). Concentrations falling within the criteria and thresholds laid out in the Competition Act must be notified to the HCA. Concentrations falling within the criteria and thresholds laid out in the European Merger Control Regulation must be notified to the European Commission and will be handled under the European Merger Control Regulation.

[183] Acquiring control in entities holding a license issued by the Hungarian energy regulatory authority may be subject to the prior approval of that regulator too. Furthermore, laws regulating the financial/insurance sector may require a notification to the Hungarian financial regulator as well with respect to changes in the controlling relationships of regulated entities.

[184] Finally, the HCA must obtain the prior consent of the National Media and Infocommunications Authority for clearing certain concentrations in the media sector.

[185] Notification is mandatory. A clear prohibition against 'jumping the gun' is in effect in respect of concentrations notifiable under the mandatory notification threshold both under the Competition Act and under the European Merger Control Regulation. The prohibition of implementation (exercising voting rights, appointing officials, etc., by the purchaser) does not affect the right to sign the transaction agreement or take any other necessary action under that agreement, provided that the concentration is not implemented. However, concentrations meeting only section 24(4) Threshold of the Competition Act (*see* below) are not subject to the suspension obligation and there is no fine for not notifying them and/or implementing them without clearance. Therefore, in practice, notification under this threshold is voluntary, but the HCA may launch an investigation ex officio within six months.

9.2 Scope of the Controls

[186] A transaction must be notified to the HCA if:

(i) *the transaction does not need to be notified to the European Commission*. Even if a transaction qualifies as a concentration and meets the thresholds below, it is not subject to notification to the HCA if it must be notified to the European Commission under the European Merger Control Regulation. In such a case, the transaction is reviewed by the European Commission only;

(ii) *the transaction constitutes a* concentration. Under the Competition Act, a *concentration* arises where: (a) two or more previously independent undertakings merge, or one merges into another, or a part of an undertaking becomes a part of another undertaking that is independent of the first undertaking; or (b) one undertaking acquires sole (or more undertakings acquire joint) direct or indirect control over an undertaking or several undertakings previously independent of the acquirer(s), but not of each other; or (c) several independent undertakings jointly set up an undertaking to be controlled by them that is capable of performing on a lasting basis all the functions of an autonomous economic entity (so-called full-function joint venture). Certain transactions performed by certain investment entities listed in the Competition Act (e.g., banks, insurance companies, and other financial institutions) which give rise only to a temporary acquisition of control do not constitute a concentration and are thus not subject to the requirement to notify the HCA.

Certain financing deals related to the COVID-19 pandemic which grant only investment protection rights to the State also do not need to be notified;

(iii) *the turnover* thresholds *are met*. There are two sets of thresholds:

(a) The Mandatory Notification Thresholds:

(1) the aggregate net turnover of all groups of undertakings concerned; and undertakings jointly controlled by a group of undertakings concerned and other undertakings (joint ventures) exceeded HUF20 bn (approximately EUR53.16 m) in the preceding business year; *and*

(2) there are at least two groups of undertakings concerned whose net sales turnover in the preceding business year – together with the proportionate net turnover of undertakings jointly controlled by the undertakings concerned and other independent undertakings – each exceeded HUF1.5 bn (approximately EUR3.98 m). Concentrations not subject to a notification requirement implemented within the preceding two years between the seller's and the purchaser's groups must be taken into account for the purpose of calculating such HUF1.5 bn thresholds.

(b) Section 24(4) HCA may be notified (on a voluntary basis) on concentrations not exceeding the above thresholds if:

(1) it is not obvious that the concentration does not substantially decrease competition in the relevant market, especially through creating or strengthening a dominant position;

(2) *and* the aggregate net turnover of all groups of undertakings concerned, together with that of the undertakings jointly controlled by a group of undertakings concerned and other independent undertakings (joint ventures), exceed HUF5 bn (approximately EUR13.29 m) in the preceding business year.

For the purpose of the net turnover calculation, the following should be observed: (i) VAT and intra-group sales must be disregarded; (ii) only the net turnover generated by goods sold or services rendered in Hungary is taken into account; (iii) special turnover calculation rules apply to credit institutions and insurance companies; (iv) the turnover of joint ventures is attributed proportionately to each controlling group.

(iv) Even if a concentration meets the thresholds, it does not need to be notified if the Government classifies that in a decree as a transaction having significance for the national economy;

(v) *the transaction is not of national strategic importance*. The Hungarian government may qualify some concentrations as having national strategic importance; such transactions are not notifiable to the HCA.

9.3 Process/Mechanics

[187] The notification procedure can be characterized as follows.

9.3.1 Notifying Parties and Notification Deadline

[188] The transactions subject to HCA merger control must be notified to the HCA:

(i) in the case of a merger by acquisition or consolidation: by all of the merging undertakings;
(ii) in the case of the establishment of a full-function joint venture: by the parent undertakings acquiring joint control; and
(iii) in the case of the acquisition of an undertaking or a part of an undertaking: by the acquiring undertaking or its directly controlling parent company.

[189] There is no general filing deadline, but the concentration cannot be implemented prior to obtaining the clearance if the mandatory notification threshold is met.

9.3.2 Pre-notification

[190] The pre-notification process may be initiated by the parties if the conclusion of the transaction has already been decided on. This does not mean that the parties must produce a signed contract or a memorandum of understanding but they must demonstrate that their intentions are sufficiently firm and definite.

[191] On the basis of the HCA's notice on pre-notification, the HCA generally requires the parties to initiate the process at least two weeks before filing the merger notification. The HCA also requires that the pre-notification be properly prepared (e.g., with a draft notification form), that the structure of the transaction should be final, and that the parties act in good faith and on a best-knowledge basis. The purpose of the pre-notification is to resolve the parties' doubts on any question that may reasonably arise with respect to the merger notification (i.e., any legal issues that are unclear in spite of the parties' adequate knowledge of the HCA's merger notification process, EU and Hungarian case law, etc.). This also means that the parties must prepare a merger control assessment themselves prior to the pre-notification, must identify any open issues, and can request consultation only on those issues.

9.3.3 Notification

[192] The merger filing must be submitted by completing the form published on the HCA's website. The scope of information to be supplied depends mainly on the market shares of the participants (i.e., whether materially overlapping or materially related markets can be identified).

[193] The notification fee is HUF1 m (approximately EUR2 656). If the HCA does not launch simplified proceedings following the notification, only the notification fee is payable. If the HCA opens a procedure, an additional HUF4 m (approximately EUR10 625) must be paid for simplified proceedings. For full proceedings, altogether HUF19 m (approximately EUR50 470) must be paid (including the above fees).

[194] Upon the filing of the notification, the HCA publishes on its website a short summary of the transaction (prepared by the notifying parties).

9.3.4 Request to Exercise Control Rights Prior to Clearance

[195] A transaction falling under the mandatory notification threshold must not be implemented prior to clearance (i.e., controlling rights arising from the transaction must not be exercised) unless the HCA's permission for exercising control before clearance has been requested and obtained. The notifying party or parties may seek the HCA's permission to exercise control rights prior to clearance if they can prove to the HCA that this is required to prevent the devaluation of the investment or other losses or damage. The HCA may make such permission subject to certain conditions limiting controlling rights. Such a request cannot be submitted during the eight days' initial review period and there are strict deadlines for making the request later in the procedure.

9.4 The Procedure for Assessment and Approval/ Rejection of Prospective or Concluded Deals

[196] The HCA decides within eight days from the receipt of the full notification (including the payment of the HUF1 m notification fee) whether to launch proceedings ex officio or not. If the HCA does not launch a procedure within this deadline, it issues an official certificate, and the concentration can be implemented.

[197] If the notification does not comply with the Competition Act or involving the National Media and Infocommunications Authority is necessary, the HCA will (subject to the payment of an additional HUF4 m procedural fees) launch a simplified procedure. The deadline for these proceedings is thirty days from the full notification. Finally, the HCA may decide to open full proceedings. The length of the full proceedings is four months, which can be extended once by an additional maximum of two months.

[198] The deadline is also four months for investigations under section 24 (4) Thresholds. These proceedings cannot be launched after six months have passed since the implementation of the concentration.

[199] The deadline is six months if the prohibition on implementation without/prior to clearance was breached or if full proceedings were not ordered due to the parties misrepresenting important facts or failing to supply important information. This deadline can be extended by a maximum of two months.

[200] The HCA's deadline will stop running when the HCA issues an information request until the information is provided. In the event the HCA fails to adopt a

decision within the statutory deadline, the clearance must be deemed to have been granted. In practice, clearance by such 'non-opposition' is extremely rare:

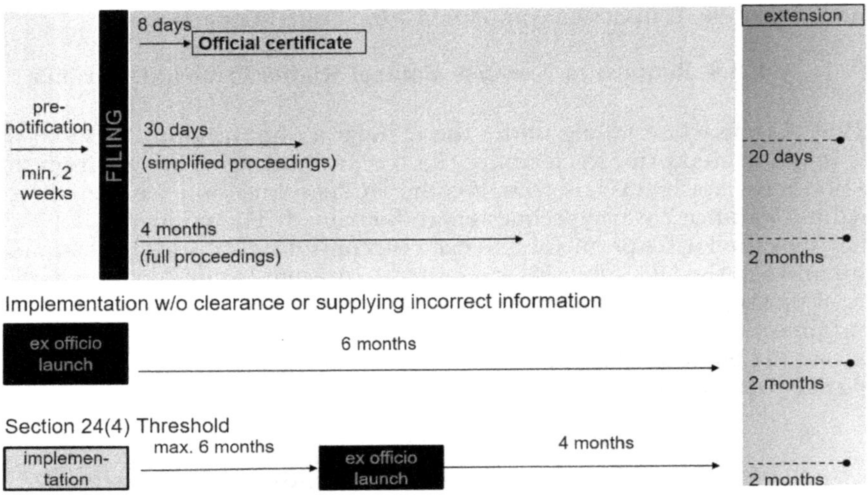

[201] In the course of merger control proceedings, the HCA evaluates the potential advantages and disadvantages arising from the merger in question, and (i) grants its unconditional clearance if the concentration does not significantly lessen competition in the relevant markets (e.g., by creating or strengthening a dominant position), or (ii) clears the transaction subject to *ex ante* or *ex post* structural or behavioural remedies, or (iii) prohibits the concentration if the requirements for granting clearance are not met. Compliance with remedies will be subsequently checked by the HCA.

[202] The final decision of the HCA may be appealed by the notifying party or parties before the court.

[203] It is possible and indeed recommended, to make use of the pre-notification process and other opportunities to engage personally with the HCA if a complicated legal problem emerges. These consultations may reduce the length of the proceedings. It is important to provide all the necessary data to the HCA in a timely manner. Finally, the HCA's notice on pre-notification states that the HCA expects lawyers representing the parties to know the rules and the case law applicable to merger control. Therefore, appointing a lawyer specialized in competition law is likely to expedite the merger clearance procedure.

9.5 What Deals Are Likely to Be Refused/Rejected?

[204] The Competition Act applies the SLC test (significantly lessening of competition), with special consideration paid to the creation or reinforcement of a dominant position. In practice, the HCA has prohibited very few deals in the past. In a number of such cases, the HCA had to prohibit the merger because the National Media and Infocommunications Authority refused to grant its consent.

9.6 Third-Party Views

[205] If the HCA decides that potential competition concerns cannot be ruled out and as a result, opens full proceedings, the HCA will, as a rule, contact third parties with information requests (especially competitors and customers/suppliers of the merging entities). Such third parties may also voluntarily submit comments to the HCA since the HCA publishes on its website the fact that a merger filing has been filed and a short description of the proposed transaction. The HCA will try to clear contradictory information (if any) received from the notifying party and third parties.

[206] Under the Competition Act, acceptable remedies include structural remedies – in particular, the divestiture of a business – and behavioural remedies. The HCA prefers structural remedies, but behavioural remedies are also commonly used to address essential facility issues. Other behavioural remedies used in the past included the separation of activities and – exceptionally – commitments regarding price or quality.

[207] Although the concentration cannot be implemented without clearance, this has no bearing on the purchaser's right to acquire the shares of a publicly held company. However, voting rights relating to such shares must not be exercised before clearance.

9.6.1 Sanctions for Breaching the Merger Control or Other Antitrust Laws

Fines

[208] In the event of implementing a concentration subject to the mandatory notification threshold in the absence of a notification to the HCA or prior to clearance, the HCA can impose on any party subject to the merger notification obligation a periodic fine amounting to a maximum of HUF300 000 (approximately EUR775) per day, starting from the earliest of the following:

- publication of the invitation to bid; or
- conclusion of the contract; or
- the acquisition of controlling rights,
  until the date of the filing or, failing this, on which the HCA launches ex officio the merger control procedure.

[209] A fine can also be imposed if the concentration is implemented in spite of a prohibition decision by the HCA, or if the commitments imposed in the conditional clearance decision were violated, or if the concentration was implemented before the pending conditions imposed were fulfilled.

[210] The fine imposed cannot exceed 13% of the annual net turnover in the preceding business year of each party or parties (or their group) subject to the notification obligation. No fine can be imposed if a concentration subject to section 24(4) Threshold is implemented without clearance.

Procedural fines

[211] A procedural fine amounting to at least HUF200 000 (approximately EUR530) and up to 1% of the preceding business year's net turnover may be imposed if the HCA grants permission to the notifying parties to exercise controlling rights prior to clearance subject to certain conditions and these conditions are breached, or if proceedings were not launched by the HCA because the parties' notification failed to communicate or misrepresented important information. Procedural fines can also be imposed on individuals.

Nullity

[212] Should the HCA prohibit a concentration implemented without clearance, the sanction will be the nullity of any action taken or deal concluded as a result of the concentration. The undertaking that acquired control in breach of merger control rules cannot invoke this nullity and will be responsible for any damage caused to third parties by the nullity.

Dawn raids

[213] While not strictly speaking a sanction, the HCA may conduct dawn raids in case of a suspected violation of the suspension obligation or the provision of false or misleading information to the HCA.

9.6.2 Anti-competitive Restraints

[214] Under the Competition Act, a decision clearing a concentration is deemed to cover restrictions directly related to and necessary for the implementation of the concentration. The HCA generally follows the practice of the European Commission on ancillary restraints.

[215] Non-compete clauses, including non-solicitation clauses, are justified by the legitimate objective of implementing the concentration when their duration, the geographical scope of their application, their subject matter and the persons subject to them do not exceed what is reasonably necessary to achieve that end. As a general rule, ancillary restraints are lawful only if they protect the purchaser, not the vendor.

[216] The duration, subject matter and geographical scope of the application of the restraint cannot exceed the extent reasonably required by the implementation of the concentration. Generally, the restriction cannot go beyond the territory and activities of the target and may last usually for three years.

[217] An employee cannot be prevented from leaving, but a non-compete agreement may be negotiated under employment laws. Such agreements can impose a non-compete obligation for a period of up to two years after the employee has left the employer and must offer fair compensation. An agreement stipulating damages in the event of a breach of the non-compete obligation may be concluded with a leaving employee to the effect that he or she will not try to solicit other employees.

9.6.3 Constraints Affecting Competitive Behaviour

[218] The main constraints affecting competitive behaviour after the deal has been concluded are the prohibition against unfair competition, anti-competitive agreements and abuse of dominance. These are regulated in the Competition Act as well as national and EU block exemption regulations. National block exemption regulations include Government decrees no. 467/2023 (X.12.) on specialization agreements, no. 204/2011 (X.7.) on motor vehicle aftermarket activity, no. 306/2022 (VII.11.) on certain vertical restraints and no. 456/2023 (X.5.) on certain research and development agreements.

[219] The HCA is also competent to deal with certain consumer protection issues which have a bearing on competition.

[220] The relevant authority to enforce antitrust law in Hungary is the HCA, which exercises effective enforcement and imposes increasingly large fines on violators. Further, parties whose rights and obligations are affected can also bring an action in court and enforce competition laws directly before the courts.

10 TAXATION ASPECTS

10.1 Nature of the Tax Regime

[221] The tax regulatory environment in Hungary is relatively certain. In general, significant changes to tax laws are introduced once a year while basic taxation concepts remain unchanged for a longer period of time.

[222] Due to budgetary reasons, however, special taxes were introduced for specific (non-manufacturing) business sectors like financial services, energy and telecommunication and from July 2014 also on certain advertisement activities (the advertisement tax is currently suspended, i.e., from 1 July 2019 until 31 December 2024), and in 2020 tax on retail activity was also introduced. On 4 June 2022, a new type of tax was introduced as extra profit surtaxes in a Government Decree.

[223] Hungary aims to be a tax-efficient jurisdiction with relatively low tax rates for corporate income (9%) and a heavier burden on VAT (27% general rate). The tax system attracts R&D activity (tax incentives and double deduction of R&D expenses) and is favourable for IPs as well (exemption on gains from IP transfer, 50% exemption of license revenues).

[224] The tax authority is relatively aggressive in enforcing tax laws with a particular focus on transfer pricing and VAT.

[225] A binding ruling system and Advanced Pricing Arrangement (APA) regime concerning transfer pricing are available.

10.2 Liability to Tax

10.2.1 General Overview

[226] This chapter provides a brief overview of the main features of the Hungarian tax system. The current main structure of the Hungarian tax system is as follows:

(i) direct taxes (e.g., corporate income tax, personal income tax);
(ii) indirect taxes (e.g., VAT);
(iii) other national taxes (e.g., stamp duty, innovation tax);
(iv) local taxes (e.g., local business tax, property tax); and
(v) special taxes (e.g., tax on the financial sector, tax on the energy sector).

10.2.2 Corporate Income Tax (CIT)

Resident entities

[227] Hungarian resident entities are subject to CIT on their worldwide income (unlimited tax liability). Normally, an entity will be regarded as a Hungarian tax resident for CIT purposes if: (a) it is incorporated under Hungarian laws, or (b) its place of management is in Hungary.

Non-resident entities

[228] Non-resident entities are taxable only up to the income that is attributable to the Hungarian permanent establishment of the foreign enterprise (limited tax liability).

[229] Capital gains realized by a foreign entity on the transfer of shareholding of a real estate holding company are subject to CIT in Hungary unless treaty protection is available.

Tax base and tax rate

[230] The CIT base equals the pre-tax profit adjusted by certain tax base increasing and decreasing items.

[231] The CIT rate is 9%.

CIT on profit minimum

[232] Provided that the pre-tax profit or the CIT base (whichever is higher) does not reach the so-called profit minimum amounting to 2% of the adjusted revenues, taxpayers are obliged to pay CIT on the basis of the profit minimum unless they make a declaration in their CIT return on a negative pre-tax profit/CIT base and do not pay any CIT.

10.2.3 VAT

[233] VAT laws are harmonized within the European Union by Council Directive 2006/112/EC of 28 November 2006 on the common system of value-added tax.

[234] The standard VAT rate is 27% whereas reduced VAT rates of 18% and 5% apply in certain cases (e.g., 18% in the case of certain food products and 5% for books, etc.).

10.2.4 Transfer Tax

General considerations

[235] Transfer tax is levied, amongst others, on the transfer of (i) real estate property, (ii) shares in real estate holding companies. A company qualifies as a real estate holding company if more than 75% of its total assets (excluding cash, receivables, accruals, and loan receivables) indicated in its financial statements consists of real estate or if it has at least a 75% direct or indirect shareholding in another company that satisfies this criterion.

[236] When transferring real estate property or shares in real estate property holding companies, the rate of the transfer tax is 4% up to a market value of HUF1 bn (approximately EUR2.5 m) and 2% in excess. The transfer tax is capped at HUF200 m (approximately EUR508 000) per real estate asset.

[237] The purchaser of shares in a real estate holding company is obliged to pay transfer tax on the acquisition once the purchaser acquires (by itself or together with its related parties) at least 75% shareholding in the real estate holding company.

Related party exemption

[238] The transfer of real estate or the shares of a real estate holding company between related parties is exempt from transfer tax under certain conditions.[1] As a

[1] The purchaser is only eligible for any exemption from transfer tax if it issues a declaration that it is not a tax resident of a country where:

- the quotient of the amount of tax and the tax base is less than half of the corporate tax rate of the parent company (i.e., less than 4.5% in the case of a direct or indirect Hungarian parent company);
- in the event that profit and tax bases are zero or negative, the amount of tax equivalent to CIT is less than 4.5% (in the country of tax residence of the purchaser);

precondition of exemption concerning the transfer of real estate between related parties, at least 50% of the purchaser's net turnover in the previous tax year shall be lease, management of own or leased real estate or the sale of own real estate.

Exemption related to preferential transactions

[239] The acquisition of any assets in the course of a preferential transformation, preferential exchange of shares or the acquisition of any real estate or shareholding in a real estate holding company in the course of a preferential transfer of assets is exempt from transfer tax under certain conditions.[2]

10.2.5 Innovation Tax

[240] Innovation tax is levied on resident companies and the permanent establishment (including branch) of the foreign company within the meaning of the Hungarian Local Tax Act. The tax rate is 0.3%. The taxable base equals the turnover adjusted by certain items.

10.2.6 Local Business Tax (Municipal Tax)

[241] Municipalities are authorized to levy local business tax on corporate taxpayers with a registered seat or permanent establishment within the territory of the municipality. The local business tax is levied on the adjusted turnover at the maximum rate of 2% (the applicable tax rate varies by municipality).

10.2.7 Building Tax (Municipal Tax)

[242] Building tax can be levied by the local municipality on buildings situated within the territory of the municipality.

[243] The taxable person is the owner of the building on the first day of the calendar year.

[244] The tax base is either the useful surface area or the adjusted fair market value of the building (subject to the discretion of the local municipality).

10.2.8 Land Tax (Municipal Tax)

[245] Land tax can be levied by the local municipality on land located within the territory of the municipality.

[246] The taxable person is the owner of the land on the first day of the year.

- income derived from the sale of shares in a real estate holding company is not subject to a tax equivalent to CIT at rates of at least 4.5% in the country of the tax residence of the purchaser.

[2] The conditions set forth in footnote No. 1 apply accordingly. The transfer tax exemption related to acquisition in the course of a preferential transfer of assets is subject to further conditions.

[247] The tax base is either the useful surface area or the adjusted fair market value of the land plot (subject to the discretion of the local municipality).

10.2.9 Other Taxes

Energy surtax

[248] The surtax is levied on certain taxpayers of the energy sector.

[249] The tax base is the pre-tax profit adjusted by certain increasing and decreasing items. The tax rate is normally 31%, however, it is temporarily increased to 41% for the year 2023 as well, with the 197/2022. (VI. 4.) Government Decree about the Extra Profit Taxes.

Telecommunication tax

[250] Telecommunication service providers are subject to tax with respect to the provision of public telecommunication services via electronic telecommunication networks located in Hungary.

[251] The telecommunication tax is based on the time of outgoing phone calls and the number of messages sent (SMS or MMS).

Advertisement tax

[252] A new surtax was introduced in Hungary in 2014 imposed on taxpayers generating income from selling media time or space displaying advertisements, and taxpayers advertising for their own benefit.

[253] However, the tax rate from 1 July 2019 until 31 December 2024 has been decreased to 0%, therefore the advertisement tax is practically suspended. It is still unknown whether the rate will be increased after this interim period or the tax itself will be revoked.

Public health product fee

[254] Such fees are imposed on the first domestic sale of products in excess of a certain sugar, salt and caffeine content (e.g., fruit and vegetable juices sold as prepackaged products, soft drinks, energy drinks, etc.).

[255] Taxable persons are the first-time sellers of taxable products in Hungary including domestic manufacturers or the first-time domestic purchaser (both in B2B and B2C relations).

[256] The tax base is the net quantity of taxable products expressed in kilograms or litres. Tax rates vary per product type (e.g., HUF390/kg on salted snacks).

Surtaxes on financial institutions

[257] Financial institutions such as banks, investment fund managers and insurance companies are subject to profit-based surtax.

[258] Payment service providers with a registered seat in Hungary are subject to financial transaction tax with respect to certain money transfers (e.g., wire transfers, cash transfers, etc.).

Extra profit surtaxes

[259] In 2022, a new Government Decree on extra profit surtaxes was introduced levying or modifying specific taxes on sectors such as mining, airlines, retail, producers subject to the compulsory purchase scheme and producers eligible for the green premium scheme covered by the KÁT and METÁR Regulations, etc.

10.2.10 Individual Taxation

General overview

Resident individuals

[260] Hungarian residents are subject to tax on their worldwide income (unlimited tax liability).[3]

Non-resident individuals

[261] Individuals other than Hungarian residents are subject to tax on their income: (i) deriving from Hungary, or (ii) taxable in Hungary based on a double tax treaty or reciprocity (limited tax liability). In general, their tax liability is assessed under the rules applicable to Hungarian residents.

Personal Income Tax (PIT) rates

[262] The general PIT rate in Hungary is 15%. This tax rate applies to all types of income subject to PIT (e.g., income derived from employment, interest income, income subject to capital gain taxation, etc.).

PAYE obligations – employment income

[263] Employment income is subject to a flat PIT rate of 15% (as described above).

---

[3] An individual is deemed to be resident in Hungary if he/she is:

(i) a Hungarian citizen, unless he/she also has dual citizenship and does not have a permanent address or residence in Hungary;
(ii) any person who exercises the right of free movement and the right of residence exceeding three months in the territory of Hungary in the calendar year in question for at least 183 calendar days, including the day of entry and the day of exit;
(iii) any person who has permanent residence status in Hungary, or is a stateless person; and
(iv) any other person not mentioned under the above paragraphs (i)–(iii) whose only permanent address is in Hungary; or whose centre of vital interests is in Hungary if he/she has no permanent address in Hungary or if Hungary is not the only country where he/she has a permanent address; or whose habitual address is in Hungary if he/she has no permanent address in Hungary or if Hungary is not the only country where he/she has a permanent address, and if his/her centre of vital interests cannot be determined.

The centre of vital interest is the country to which the individual, taking into account his/her personal, family and economic circumstances, has the closest relationship.

[264] Employment income is subject to 13% social tax (levied on the gross salary) which is to be paid by the employer to the tax authority not later than the twelfth day of the month following the month of the salary payment.

[265] Employers are obliged to deduct the PIT advance and 18.5% social security contribution from the gross monthly salary paid to the employee and to transfer the relevant amounts to the tax authority by not later than the twelfth day of the month following the month of the salary payment.

11 CAPITAL ALLOWANCES AND OTHER DEDUCTIONS

11.1 Depreciation

[266] When calculating the CIT base, accounting depreciation increases the pre-tax profit, while tax depreciation decreases the pre-tax profit.

[267] The CIT Act stipulates the depreciation rates applicable to real estate properties and fixed assets.

[268] The depreciation rate in the case of real estate properties is generally 2%. Preferential tax depreciation rates apply to particular assets (33%, 50% depreciation rate), while in the case of IP, the same depreciation rates are to be used for accounting purposes.

[269] As a special type of accelerated depreciation, taxpayers can decide to set aside a reserve (i.e., as a restricted reserve) for development purposes of up to the amount of the pre-tax profit. The amount set aside decreases the CIT base in the relevant tax year, on the one hand, while on the other hand, no tax depreciation can be utilized with respect to the asset set in operation as part of the investment up to the value of the reserve. Accordingly, the setting aside of a reserve for development purposes results in an early (accelerated) tax depreciation.

11.2 Dividend Income, Interest Expenses and IP Deductions: Corporate Income Tax Base Deductions

Dividend

[270] In general, dividend income is CIT exempt unless received from a CFC.

[271] According to the Hungarian tax laws, a CFC is a foreign entity:

> A CFC is a non-resident company that meets the following conditions.
>
> 1) A foreign entity is regarded as a CFC if a Hungarian taxpayer, either on its own or together with related entities/persons:

- holds direct or indirect participation of more than 50 per cent of the voting rights of that entity; or
- owns, directly or indirectly, more than 50 per cent of the registered capital of that entity; or
- is entitled to receive more than 50 per cent of the profits of the foreign entity;

  in the tax year in which the tax corresponding to the corporate tax actually paid by the foreign entity is less than half of the corporate tax rate of the parent company (i.e. less than 4.5 percent in the case of a direct or indirect Hungarian parent company).

[272] A resident taxpayer's foreign permanent establishment is also a CFC in the tax year in which the tax corresponding to the corporate tax paid by the foreign permanent establishment is less than 4.5%.

[273] A foreign entity or permanent establishment does not qualify as a CFC if the income of the foreign entity or permanent establishment is derived solely from a transaction (or series of transactions) regarded as genuine.

[274] CFC provisions also apply to permanent establishments of the foreign entity.

[275] The above conditions must be evidenced by the taxpayer (i.e., the burden of proof is placed on the taxpayer).

Undistributed profit of a Controlled-Foreign Company (CFC)

[276] The Hungarian CIT base must be increased by the undistributed after-tax profits of a CFC in proportion to the direct interest of the Hungarian taxpayer in the CFC under certain conditions.

Royalty deduction

[277] Fifty per cent of the revenues arising from qualifying royalties reduce the CIT base. However, such reduction may not exceed 50% of the profit before tax.

Reported intangible asset

[278] If the acquired or developed qualifying intangible asset is duly reported to the tax authority within sixty days subsequent to acquisition or development, any gains related to the sale/in-kind contribution of such assets are CIT exempt.

Non-reported intangible asset

[279] In circumstances where the acquired or developed intangible asset is not reported, additional CIT benefits can be achieved by placing the gains on the selling/in-kind contribution of such assets into the tied-up reserve which decreases the CIT base in the given year. The condition for this benefit is that within five years subsequent to the placement of such assets into the tied-up reserve, a new, royalty-bearing intangible asset is purchased from the gains placed into the reserve.

Research and development (R&D) deduction

[280] The direct costs of basic research, applied research and experimental development (conducted by the taxpayer as its own activity) accounted for as expenses are deductible twice for CIT purposes provided that it is connected with the taxpayer's business activities (i.e., double deduction is available).

[281] Taxpayers are also allowed to deduct the direct costs of basic research and experimental development if the costs are incurred by their related party. Preconditions of such deduction are that: (i) such related party did not make a deduction in this respect; and (ii) the underlying activities are related to the business activities of both entities.

[282] Benefits of the double R&D deduction can also be exploited by a '*cost-sharing agreement*' where an R&D activity is conducted outside of Hungary but the company enjoys benefits from such R&D activity.

Reported participation

[283] If the taxpayer reports the acquisition of shareholding in a domestic or foreign entity to the tax authority within seventy-five days and holds such shares for at least one year, any gains realized on the sale/in-kind contribution of such shares is CIT exempt. This rule does not apply to a shareholding in a CFC (however impairment loss and capital loss on reported participation is non-deductible).

11.3 Development Tax Allowance (DTA): Deduction from the Corporate Income Tax Payable

[284] Taxpayers investing or creating new jobs in Hungary may be entitled to a development tax credit (i.e., an indirect state aid) which can be used up to 80% of their CIT due per annum.

[285] The availability and the amount of tax credit depends on the location, value (i.e., eligible costs) and type of investment. The maximum aid intensity should be considered in each case. The development tax credit may be utilized during various tax years.

[286] DTA can be available with respect to investments with a present value of at least HUF3 bn; investments in the territory of a prioritized municipality with a present value of at least HUF1 bn or with respect to the creation of new jobs as a result of a new investment. Investments with a present value of at least HUF100 m concerning – amongst others – environmental and R&D investments can also be eligible for a DTA

[287] As an implementation of the new general block exemption regulation of the European Commission effective from 1 July 2014, several changes were introduced to the Hungarian DTA legislation restricting the availability of a DTA for large enterprises in the Central Region of Hungary.

12 TAX CONSOLIDATION: GROUP RELIEF OF GAINS AND LOSSES

12.1 Group Taxation for CIT Purposes

[288] From 2019, Hungarian resident companies may opt for group taxation, if the following conditions are met: (i) the members of the group are linked by at least 75% of the voting rights; (ii) have identical balance sheet dates; and (iii) the same rules of reporting or bookkeeping (according to IFRS or Hungarian rules). Group taxation has to be requested before the end of a year by at least two companies and has to be approved by the tax administration. The group CIT base is the total of the positive tax bases of the individual members, which may be reduced by the losses carried forward by the companies in the group. In a CIT group, intra-group transactions are exempt from transfer pricing obligations.

12.2 Indirect Non-CFC Subsidiary Loss Relief

[289] As an indirect foreign loss relief, any impairment incurred with respect to a shareholding in a foreign subsidiary (which is not a CFC) is deductible for CIT purposes.[4]

12.3 Unused Tax Losses

[290] Losses of a given tax year can be carried forward in the subsequent five tax years at the taxpayer's election.

[291] Losses carried forward from previous tax years may only be used to decrease the pre-tax profit up to 50% of the CIT base.

[292] Utilization of losses carried forward in the case of corporate restructurings and preferential transfer of assets are subject to certain limitations.

13 TAX CONSIDERATIONS ARISING ON M&A TRANSACTIONS

[293] This section provides a brief overview of the:

(i) tax considerations of share deals and assets deals (considering implications for both corporate and individual taxpayers);

[4] However, any write-back of impairment with respect to a shareholding in a non-CFC company is taxable resulting from a significant and permanent increase in the value of the shareholding compared to its book value.

(ii) brief summary on valuation/determination of transaction prices;
(iii) tax considerations related to the structuring of an investment;
(iv) possible tax clearance methods available in Hungary.

13.1 Tax Considerations of Share Deals

[294] It is assumed that both the vendor and the purchaser are domestic taxpayers. Where required, the analysis also covers the tax consequences related to a foreign vendor/purchaser.

[295] It is also assumed that all transactions are made in exchange for consideration:

A) Tax considerations (Corporate taxpayers)		
Taxes	*Vendor*	*Purchaser*
Corporate Income Tax (CIT)	**Domestic vendor (sale of shares)** – In general, gains realized on the sale of shares are taxable for CIT purposes (tax rate 9%). – The gains realized on the sale of so-called *reported participation*[5] are not taxable for CIT purposes unless the participation in a CFC[6] is sold. – In general, any losses incurred on the sale of shares are recognized expenses, if they relate to business-like and revenue-generating activity. Losses incurred on the sale of a reported participation are non-recognized losses.	*(The below is only applicable to resident purchasers)* – In general, acquisition expenses are deductible for CIT purposes, provided that they are incurred with respect to business-like and revenue-generating activity. – The purchase of shares does not trigger any CIT. – The purchaser is entitled to report the shares acquired to the tax authority (within a deadline of seventy-five days) in order to qualify for the '*reported participation*' exemption. – The amount of consideration paid for the shares is (i) either to be accounted as shares and participations or (ii) partly as shares and

[5] Please *see* our description in s. 3.2.
[6] *See* the definition of a CFC in s. 3.2.

	– Losses carried forward decrease the CIT base by up to 50% of the positive CIT base (in a time limit of five tax years). – Non-realized FX gains on shares denominated in a currency other than the bookkeeping currency crystallize upon the sale. **Domestic vendor (share for share transaction)** – CIT consequences of share for share transactions may incur at the level of quotaholders/shareholders. – In the case of an in-kind contribution above book value, the capital gains are in general taxable for CIT purposes. Losses incurred due to an in-kind contribution below book value, are recognized losses. – Taxation on capital gains can be deferred if the transaction qualifies as a *'preferential exchange of shares'*.[7] If so,	participations and partly as goodwill.[8] Ordinary depreciation of goodwill is available and goodwill impairment is available, in principle, which may be tax deductible. – If the shares acquired are denominated in a currency other than the bookkeeping currency then such investment is subject to revaluation on the balance sheet date that may result in non-realized FX gains or losses. – If non-realized FX gains or losses arise, this shall be booked as other financial income/expense, where the gains are in general taxable. However, the purchaser has the option to defer taxation until the long-term financial instrument is actually written-off from its books (due to sale, impairment, etc.). Once the financial instrument is written-off, non-realized and deferred FX gains or losses must be recaptured and the CIT base is to be increased/decreased accordingly. – Impairment losses on shares are deductible for accounting purposes. For CIT purposes, impairment loss on CFC shares and reported

[7] The conditions to be met are the following:

– a company (the acquiring company) acquires an interest in the share capital of another company (the acquired company) In return for the acquired share capital, the acquiring company's shareholders also acquire shares in the acquiring company;

A) Tax considerations (Corporate taxpayers)		
Taxes	*Vendor*	*Purchaser*
	capital gains will become taxable only when the shares acquired are written-off from the books, e.g., due to sale, capital decrease, contribution in-kind (unless made in the form of an additional preferential exchange of shares). – Taxation of non-realized FX gains that would normally crystallize at the time of the write-off can also be deferred in preferential exchange of shares. ---------------------------	participation are not deductible. Impairment which did not incur in the course of the acquirer's business-like and revenue-generating activity is also non-deductible for CIT purposes. – The write-back of any impairment can be subject to CIT.[9]

- the acquiring company may also make a cash payment to the acquired company's shareholders, but only up to 10% of the nominal value of the shares issued (in the absence of a nominal value, up to 10% of the book value);
- the acquiring company must acquire a majority of the voting rights in the acquired company; and
- the shareholders of the acquired company must keep separate records of all shares acquired in the preferential transaction.

[8] If less than 75% of voting rights are acquired, the acquisition value of the shares is the amount of consideration. If more than 75% of the voting rights are acquired, the part of the consideration proportionate to the market value of the equity of the acquired company is accounted for as shares and participations, the part in excess of the latter amount is accounted as goodwill.

[9] Due that only 50% of deferred losses from previous tax years can be taken into account as to offset any revenues realized through the write-back of impairment.

	Foreign vendor (sale or share for share transaction) – The sale of shares by a foreign vendor which has no permanent establishment in Hungary is, in general, not subject to tax in Hungary. – The transfer (e.g., sale or capital reduction) of shares in a 'real estate property holding company' is subject to CIT in Hungary unless treaty protection is provided.	
Tax losses	– The taxpayer loses its right to use its previously incurred tax in the case of a merger, division or transformation, if the majority ownership of the successor entity changes, or if the successor entity does not continue at least one of the predecessor entities' activities in the two tax years following the merger, division or transformation. The taxpayer loses its right to use its previously incurred tax losses if direct or indirect majority influence over the company is acquired by another taxpayer who (or whose legal predecessor) was not a related party to the taxpayer (or its legal predecessor). – The above restrictions do not apply if (i) either the taxpayer or the acquiring entity is listed on a regulated market at the time of acquisition; or (ii) the taxpayer continues its activity for two consecutive tax years following the acquisition of the majority influence and the nature of the activity is not materially different from that of the activity pursued prior to the acquisition and the taxpayer generates revenues from that activity in both tax years.	
Transfer pricing (TP)	– In principle, Hungarian transfer pricing provisions follow the OECD Trans fer Pricing Guidelines.	– TP rules require taxpayers (i) to adjust their CIT base if the prices applied in related party transactions are not at arm's length and (ii) to prepare a TP documentation for transactions reaching a certain threshold.

A) Tax considerations (Corporate taxpayers)		
Taxes	*Vendor*	*Purchaser*
	– TP rules require taxpayers to adjust their CIT base if the prices applied in related party[10] transactions are not at arm's length. – TP adjustments are made irrespective of other tax-base increasing or decreasing items. For instance, if the interest deduction rule applies in the case of a company and applies a higher interest rate than the market one, it has to increase its CIT based on both grounds. – Further, in general, to support the arm's-length nature of prices applied in related party transactions, taxpayers are obliged to prepare transfer pricing documentation. – Such documentation should be prepared by the date of filing the CIT return.	

[10] Related party means:
(a) the taxpayer and the person in which the taxpayer has a majority interest – whether directly or indirectly – according to the applicable legal provisions;

Value added tax (VAT)	– The sale of shares should not trigger any VATable event in Hungary (however, certain administrative requirements may apply).	–
Transfer tax	–	– In general, the acquisition of shares is not subject to transfer tax. However, the acquisition of shares in a real estate holding company[11] can be subject to transfer tax (also for foreign taxpayers).

(b) the taxpayer and the person that has a majority interest in the taxpayer – whether directly or indirectly – according to the applicable legal provisions;
(c) the taxpayer and another person if a third party has a majority interest in both the taxpayer and such other person – whether directly or indirectly – according to the applicable legal provisions;
(d) a foreign enterprise and its domestic place of business and the business premises of the foreign enterprise, furthermore, the domestic place of business of a foreign enterprise and the person who is in the relationship defined under points a)–c) with the foreign enterprise;
(e) the taxpayer and its foreign establishment, and the taxpayer's foreign establishment and the person who has a relationship with the taxpayer as defined under points a)–c),
(f) the taxpayer and another person if there is a decisive influence on the business and financial policy of the taxpayer due to management consistency.

[11] *See* hereto our further analysis at s. 2.4.

B) Tax considerations (individual taxpayers)		
Taxes	*Vendor*	*Purchaser*
Personal Income Tax (PIT)	Domestic vendor (sales of shares) – In general, capital gains realized on the sale of shares are taxable for PIT purposes. – The income is the amount received less the certified costs in relation to the acquisition and holding of the shares. – Due to that no loss carry-forward concept is available for the sale of shares by private individuals, capital gains cannot be offset by capital losses of previous tax years (except in special cases where transactions are made via the financial service provider or broker). – Sale of shares in a company resident in low tax measure state qualifies as other income and is subject to 15% PIT and is subject to 13% social tax. Low tax measure state means states with no CIT obligation or with tax measure under 9%, except there is a double tax treaty between the state and Hungary. Domestic vendor (share for share transaction) – In the case of an in-kind contribution, the market value of shares acquired (less acquisition value) as a result of in-kind contribution is taxable for PIT purposes. – Similar to corporate shareholders, taxation can be deferred if the transaction qualifies as a '*preferential exchange of shares*'.[12] -	– The fair market value of the acquired shares in excess of the acquisition cost is taxable for PIT purposes. – Where the transfer takes place between independent parties, the fair market value is the price they apply in the transaction (hence no taxable income should arise). – Where the transfer takes place between non-independent parties,[13] the fair market value is to be determined in line with special provisions. – No taxable income should arise in certain cases, e.g., when the purchaser acquires the shares from another private individual and the price reaches at least the face value or when the shares are acquired by the way of capital increase from the equity of the company. – The cost of acquiring shares will be taken into account when calculating the income on the sale of such shares as a decreasing item.

[12] The conditions to be met are the following:

- a company (the acquiring company) acquires an interest in the share capital of another company (the acquired company). In return for the acquired share capital, the acquiring company issues shares to the shareholders of the acquired company;
- the acquiring company may also make a cash payment to the acquired company's shareholders, but only up to 10% of the nominal value of the shares issued (in the absence of a nominal value, up to 10% of the book value);

	Foreign vendor (sale or share for share transaction) – The sale of shares by a foreign vendor is in general not subject to tax in Hungary, however, the relevant DTT rules shall be considered accordingly. – The sale of shares in a real property holding company can be subject to taxation in Hungary in the case of a foreign vendor (subject to the applicable DTT).	
Value added tax (VAT)	– The sale of shares should not trigger any VATable event in Hungary.	–
Transfer tax	–	– The purchaser (also foreign purchasers) may be subject to transfer tax if shares of a real estate holding company are acquired.[14]

– the acquiring company must acquire a majority of the voting rights in the acquired company; and
– the shareholders of the acquired company must keep separate records of all shares acquired in the preferential transaction.

[13] Those persons are non-independent (private individuals, legal entities and other organizations) who have such close legal or economic relationship due to which one of them has a governing influence over the other party's business decisions or under which the parties operate in close cooperation (non-independent parties are, in particular, the parties to an employment relationship or the majority shareholder of a company and the company).

[14] *See also* at s. 2.4.

13.2 Tax Considerations Related to Asset Deals

A) Tax considerations (Corporate taxpayers)		
Taxes	*Vendor*	*Purchaser*
Corporate Income Tax (CIT)	**Domestic vendor (sale of assets)** – If the sale price of the asset is higher than its book value then such profit is in general taxable for CIT purposes. – Differences in the tax value and the accounting value of the assets can result in CIT liability. – The profits realized on the sale of a '*reported intangible property*' are not taxable for CIT purposes[15] under certain conditions. – In general, any losses incurred on the sale of assets are recognized expenses, if they relate to business-like and revenue-generating activity. **Domestic vendor (in-kind contribution)** – Where assets are contributed in-kind to the capital of another company above book value the profits are in general	– In general, acquisition expenses are deductible for CIT purposes, provided that they incur with respect to business-like and revenue-generating activity. – Provided that the acquisition of intangible property is duly reported to the tax authority within sixty days subsequent to acquisition the profits realized are exempt from CIT. – Upon the acquisition of a business unit goodwill may be recorded at the purchaser. Impairment loss on goodwill is, in principle, tax deductible and ordinary straight-line depreciation is also tax deductible.

[15] *See also* at s. 3.2.

	taxable for CIT purposes. Losses incurred due to an in-kind contribution below book value, are recognized losses. Tax loss carry-forward is available up to 50% of the CIT base (losses can be carried forward within five tax years). – Taxation can be deferred if the transfer qualifies as a '*preferential transfer of assets*'.[16]	
Transfer pricing (TP)	– The Transfer pricing considerations outlined in section 5.1. apply accordingly.	– Transfer pricing considerations outlined in section 5.1. apply accordingly.

[16] The conditions for a 'preferential transfer of assets' are met if:

- the seller company transfers without being dissolved one or more of its business units to the acquiring company. In exchange, the seller company receives shares forming part of the share capital of the acquiring company;
- the seller transferred a business unit (meaning all of the assets and liabilities of a separate organizational division of the seller company that could be operative on its own);
- the acquirer and seller company entered into an agreement which contains an itemized list of the transferred assets and liabilities, indicating their original acquisition cost and book value for the date of transfer. The agreement must also contain the acquiring company's commitment that after the transaction it will determine its taxable base (taking into consideration the assets and liabilities received from the seller) as if the transfer had not taken place;
- the seller company notifies the tax authorities of its election of the preferential transfer of assets. This notification is included in the tax return of the year of transfer;
- the acquiring company maintained separate records on the revalued assets and liabilities. These must contain the acquisition cost, book value for both accounting and tax purposes on the date of transfer and all of the adjusting items of the pre-tax profit applied with regard to these assets and liabilities after the transfer; and
- the transfer is based on real commercial, economic reasons, to be proved by the taxpayer.

A) Tax considerations (Corporate taxpayers)		
Taxes	*Vendor*	*Purchaser*
Tax losses	– Where a business transfer is implemented as a 'preferential transfer of assets' the tax losses attributed to such business can be transferred together with the business and can be used by the transferee under certain conditions.	
Value added tax (VAT)	**Domestic vendor (sale of assets)** – The sale of assets is in general subject to VAT at various rates (predominantly 27%). – The transfer of assets can be out of the scope of VAT if they are transferred as a '*going concern*' subject to certain conditions.[17]	**Domestic purchaser (purchase of assets)** – If VAT is charged by the vendor (or in the case of reverse-charge VAT), the purchaser can deduct the VAT charged by the vendor unless the deduction is not available due to a special rule or non-compliance with conditions for VAT deduction.

[17] The purchaser of assets as a 'going concern': (i) shall be registered in Hungary as a taxable person at the time of acquisition or in direct consequence thereof; (ii) provide guarantees that the rights and obligations prescribed under the tax laws in connection with the assets acquired are conferred upon him at the time of acquisition; (iii) the purchaser shall not have any legal status at the time of acquisition or subsequently that, owing to its character, is incompatible with the latter guarantee provided.

Further, the economic activity conducted in the line of business is limited to the supply of goods and services entitling to VAT deduction; and if the assets acquired contain any real estate property or part of a property in respect of which, the transferee did exercise the option to tax.

	Immoveable property *a) VAT exemption* – The sale of a building (or parts of a building) and the land on which the building stands or the supply of land (or part of land) which has not been built on. *b) Reverse-charge VAT* – The taxpayer can also opt for taxation in the case of point a). – In this case, VAT is to be self-assessed by the customer who is at the same time entitled to VAT deduction (provided that the general conditions of VAT deduction are met). *c) Application of general VAT regime (VAT to be charged by the vendor)* – The selling of a building (or parts of a building) and the land on which the building stands: (i) prior to the first occupation of the property; or (ii) after the first occupation but not later than two years after the occupancy permit became final; or (iii) after the first occupation, the intended use of the property have been changed and two years have elapsed since the issue of the certificate of the change. – Supply of a building site (or part of it).	**Domestic purchaser (assets contributed in-kind)** – Transfer of assets via in-kind contribution may qualify under certain conditions as a transaction which is not subject to VAT. – If the in-kind contribution is subject to VAT, VAT deduction depends on the fulfilment of the above criteria. – As a precondition of out-of-scope treatment for VAT purposes, the purchaser is obliged to provide a guarantee concerning possible VAT obligations (applicable both for sale and in-kind contribution).

A) Tax considerations (Corporate taxpayers)		
Taxes	*Vendor*	*Purchaser*

	Domestic vendor (in-kind contribution)
	
	– The sale can be out of the scope of VAT if the following requirements are met with respect to the purchaser:
	  – the purchaser is registered in Hungary as a taxable person at the time of acquisition or in direct consequence thereof;
	  – the purchaser provides a guarantee that the rights and obligations are conferred upon him at the time of acquisition;
	  – the purchaser does not have any legal status at the time of acquisition or subsequently that, owing to its character, is incompatible with the above guarantee.
	– In addition to the above, in the case of a '*transfer of a going concern*', the following criteria should also be met:
	  – the assets transferred need to constitute a business unit that is capable of independent operation,	

	– the business unit is acquired with the aim of further operation, – the activity performed within the business unit is a VAT able activity.	
Transfer tax	–	– The acquisition of any real estate or any rights with monetary value related to real properties or motor vehicles[18] is subject to transfer tax.

[18] For the applicable transfer tax rates, *see* s. 2.4.

B) Tax considerations (individual taxpayers)		
Taxes	*Vendor*	*Purchaser*
Personal Income Tax (PIT)	**General considerations** – In general, profits realized on the sale of assets are taxable for PIT purposes (15% tax rate). Taxation follows the type of asset subject to sale and the tax qualification of the transaction (i.e., separate or aggregate taxation). – Due to that no loss carry-forward concept is available for the sale of assets by private individuals, capital gains cannot be offset by capital losses of previous tax years. – The income derived from the sale of any moveable or immovable property can be decreased by: (i) acquisition costs; (ii) value-increasing investments; (iii) costs related to the sale of the assets. – If the sale of movable or immovable property is carried out as a business activity, it can be subject to different PIT and social contribution regimes depending on the form of business activity (e.g., can be subject to tax as the profit of a private entrepreneur, etc.).	– The cost of acquiring the assets will be taken into account when calculating the income on the sale of such assets as a decreasing item.

	Moveable property – Income derived from the sale of any moveable property up to HUF600 000 can be disregarded when establishing the taxable income.[19] **Immovable property** – Subject to the relevant DTT rules, the selling of a Hungarian immovable property can result in Hungarian PIT taxation also for foreign individuals. – Tax allowance is available from the PIT depending on (a) the number of years passed after the particular asset has been acquired and (b) the type of the real estate property. No tax should be paid on the sale from the 5th year following the year of the acquisition.	
Value added tax (VAT)	**General considerations** – In general, the selling of any assets (moveable or immovable) by an individual is out of the scope of VAT.	– As an individual taxpayer, natural persons are in general not entitled to VAT deduction, unless certain conditions are met.

[19] The PIT determined related to the sale of movable property up to HUF30 000 is not payable.

B) Tax considerations (individual taxpayers)		
Taxes	*Vendor*	*Purchaser*
	Moveable property – If moveable property is sold in a business-like manner, the sale of such asset is subject to the general VAT regime with certain exemptions. **Immoveable property** *a) VAT exemption (selling in a business-like manner)* – The selling of a building (or parts of a building) and the land on which the building stands or the supply of land (or part of land) which has not been built on. *b) Reverse-charge VAT (selling in a business-like manner)* – The taxpayer can also opt for taxation in the case of point a). VAT is to be self-assessed by the purchaser (who is also entitled to VAT deduction provided that the general conditions of VAT deduction are met).	

	c) Application of general VAT regime (VAT to be charged and paid by the vendor) – selling in a business-like manner – The selling of a building (or parts of a building) and the land on which the building stands: (i) prior to the first occupation of the property; or (ii) after the first occupation but not later than two years after the occupancy permit became final; or (iii) after the first occupation, the intended use of the property have been changed and two years have elapsed since the issue of the certificate of the change. – Supply of a building land (or part of a building land). *d) Selling as a non-taxable person in a series of transactions (VAT to be charged and paid by the vendor)* – If (i) a building (or parts of a building) and the land on which the building stands or (ii) building land (parts of a building land) are sold in the course of a series of transactions[20] as a non-taxable person.	

B) Tax considerations (individual taxpayers)		
Taxes	*Vendor*	*Purchaser*
Transfer tax	–	– The purchaser (also foreign purchasers) may be subject to transfer tax in the case of acquisition of any real estate or any rights with monetary value related to real properties or motor vehicles.[21]

[20] A series of transactions shall in general mean the fourth and any subsequent sale of building land (parts of a building land) and/or building under construction or developed building land within two calendar years.

[21] *See* hereto our further analysis at s. 2.4.

13.3 Valuation/Determination of Transaction Prices

13.3.1 CIT Considerations

[296] There is no mandatory valuation requirement for CIT purposes as regards transaction pricing.

13.3.2 Transfer Pricing Considerations

[297] In the case of related party transactions, the prices applied are subject to the general transfer pricing provisions resulting in transfer pricing adjustments when applying non-arm's length prices.

13.3.3 Corporate Law Considerations

[298] In the case of in-kind contributions at companies limited by shares ('*Zrt.*' and '*Nyrt.*'), the relevant corporate laws require the in-kind contribution to be audited by an auditor or a competent expert. The aim of such an audit is to confirm whether the value indicated in the deed of foundation does not exceed the value of the actual in-kind contribution.

[299] No such mandatory valuation is required with respect to the in-kind contribution at limited liability companies ('*Kft.*'). Quotaholders accepting an in-kind contribution at a higher value than the value prevailing at the time of contribution (i.e., overvaluation) are jointly and severally liable with the quotaholder performing the in-kind contribution for damages arising out of such conduct at the level of the company.

13.4 Structuring the Investment

13.4.1 Withholding Taxes (WHT)

[300] In general, any dividends, interest, royalties, and services fees[22] (e.g., management and consultancy fees) paid to a foreign tax resident company which has no permanent establishment in Hungary are not subject to WHT in Hungary.

[301] Any dividends, interest, or royalties paid to foreign tax resident individuals are subject to WHT in Hungary.

[302] Any payments made to non-resident corporations in respect of the purchase or renting of immovable property are not subject to WHT in Hungary while withholding tax may apply where the recipient of income is a foreign resident individual

[22] Service and management fees are generally deductible for tax purposes. Service fees in an amount exceeding HUF200 000 (excluding VAT) are not deductible if it can be shown that the service was supplied without genuine business purpose.

Sale of shares in a real estate property company

[303] Gains realized by foreign tax resident entities on the sale of the shares of a Hungarian real estate holding company[23] may be subject to CIT in Hungary.

13.4.2 Debt Financing

[304] In the case of financing of an acquisition by loan, the deductibility of interest payable on such loan is subject to certain limitations for CIT purposes such as (i) interest deduction rules; (ii) transfer pricing; and (iii) the so-called business purpose test.

Interest deduction rules

[305] Based on the Hungarian CIT legislation, there is a special deduction limitation on interest expenses exceeding 30% of EBITDA of the previous tax year or HUF939 810 000 (EUR3 m) per tax year (whichever is higher). ('*interest deduction rules*').

[306] Accordingly, if the net financing costs exceed 30% of EBITDA of the previous tax year or HUF939 810 000 (EUR3 m) per tax year, then the interest on the liabilities exceeding this threshold is not deductible for CIT purposes. In addition to the above (similarly to the carrying forward of tax losses), taxpayers are allowed to carry forward the non-deductible net financing costs and utilize them (i.e., make them tax deductible), provided that the taxpayer has 'unutilized interest deduction capacity' in a certain tax year. For the purpose of 'unutilized interest deduction capacity', the difference of the 30% of the EBITDA and the net financing cost in each year should be considered. Similarly, the non-deductible net financing cost unutilized interest deduction capacity may be carried forward to future periods as well. Unutilized interest deduction capacity should be utilized in accordance with the first-in, first-out (FIFO) principle and within five years as of their generation.

[307] Income from long-term state investment and income not subject to CIT are to be disregarded when determining the EBITDA.

[308] Deemed interest in line with transfer pricing rules to be considered when determining the net financing costs (i.e., if the interest rate applied between related parties is lower than the arm's-length interest and therefore, the CIT base has to be adjusted by the difference, it also needs to be considered for interest deduction limitation purposes).

Business purpose test

[309] The business purpose test means that expenses (e.g., interest expenses) of the entity subject to CIT are incurred in relation to its business-like and revenue-generating activity. General deductibility is presumed unless costs and expenses (e.g., interest expenses) are incurred as a consideration paid to a CFC.

[23] Details to taxation of selling of shares in a real estate holding company are outlined in s. 2.4.

Transfer pricing

[310] If the application of non-arm's length interest rates in a related party transaction results in a lower pre-tax profit (i.e., the applied interest rates are higher than the market rates), the taxpayer's CIT base must be increased by the difference between the arm's length and the actually applied interest rate.

[311] In the opposite case (i.e., where a lower interest rate is applied than the market rate), the CIT base may be decreased subject to certain conditions.

13.4.3 Real Estate Investment Trust (REIT)

[312] In 2011, a REIT regime was adopted in Hungary to promote investors in the real estate sector and to potentially increase the overall amount of real estate investment.

[313] A Hungarian REIT must be established in the form of a public company limited by shares having a minimum start-up capital of HUF5 bn. The REIT may only hold SPVs fulfilling detailed requirements laid down by law. The real estate portfolio of the REIT (referring to the real estate held by the REIT and the SPVs) must amount to at least 70% of its balance sheet total.

[314] Hungarian REIT regulation prefers small investors by laying down the following criteria:

(i) total shareholdings of institutional investors (i.e., banks, insurance companies) must not exceed 10% of the issued shares;
(ii) at least 25% of the REIT's share capital must qualify as free float. In this context, free float refers to a series of shares where no shareholder holds more than 5% of the free float shares (i.e., the 5% threshold is not established based on the total number of shares);
(iii) shares at least in the amount of the free float must be introduced to a regulated market (stock exchange);
(iv) at least 90% of the profit after tax must be proposed to be distributed annually, however, the shareholders decide on whether it actually gets distributed or not.

[315] REIT status is subject to a preliminary registration by the tax authority. Subsequent to the registration, a preferential tax regime applies to REITs and their SPVs as follows:

(i) a decreased transfer tax rate of 2% applies to the direct acquisition of any real estate or shares in a '*property holding company*';
(ii) they are not subject to CIT liability (unless failing to observe the arm's-length principle in related party transactions); and
(iii) no local business tax liability applies to its business revenues.

[316] It is important to note that, despite the increasing interest of investors, only very few REITs have been established in Hungary to date.

13.4.4 Tax Clearance

[317] To gain certainty on the tax consequences of a transaction prior to its actual implementation, a binding or non-binding ruling can be requested from the relevant authorities as follows.

[318] Before submitting a non-binding ruling request, it is usually possible to liaise with the relevant authorities.

Non-binding tax ruling

[319] Taxpayers can request the Hungarian Tax Authority or the Ministry of Finance in advance to provide a preliminary, non-binding opinion on the tax consequences of the transaction (free of any administrative expenses).

Binding tax ruling

[320] Taxpayers can request an advance binding ruling from the Ministry of Finance in relation to the tax consequences of a future transaction. Under certain conditions, a binding ruling can be obtained in relation to transactions which have already been implemented.

[321] There is a ninety-day deadline to issue the binding ruling (which can be extended by an additional sixty days). A fast-track procedure is also available with a deadline of sixty days (which can be extended by a further thirty days).

[322] The regular fee for the ruling in case of a standard contract is HUF8 m and in other cases HUF10 m. If the fast-track procedure is requested, the fee is HUF12 m.

[323] The ruling issued is binding on the tax authorities until the end of the fifth tax year subsequent to the delivery of the ruling, which can be prolonged by two years, except in case of any changes in the legislation or any changes in the factual background.

[324] Advance binding rulings may not be subject to appeal but can only be challenged before the court.

[325] It is also possible to request an extension of an existing binding ruling's effect when, due to legislative changes or a material change in the factual background, the binding ruling should be deemed to be ineffective.

Advance pricing arrangement (APA)

[326] Related parties may request the tax authorities to issue an advance ruling on the transfer pricing aspects of a future transaction (i.e., the applicable transfer pricing method, the decisive facts and circumstances and, if possible, the arm's-length price).

[327] If the transaction also concerns the tax legislation of another country, the Minister must conclude an agreement with the relevant foreign authorities (i.e.,

bilateral or multilateral procedure). If such an agreement is not available, a unilateral ruling may be given at the request of the taxpayer only if the information available to the Minister is sufficient to establish an arm's length price.

[328] The deadline for issuing the APA is 120 days which can be extended twice, each time for another 60 days.[24]

[329] The APA is binding for all tax authorities unless relevant circumstances change. The APA is valid for a period of three to five years which can be extended for an additional three years.

14 EMPLOYMENT CONSIDERATIONS

14.1 Legislative Framework

[330] The most important source of law regulating employment relationships in Hungary is the Labour Code, which regulates both individual and collective labour law, as well as employment disputes.

[331] Most of the provisions contained in the Labour Code are mandatory. However, the parties to an employment relationship may agree on obligations that are different from certain requirements of the Labour Code if this is expressly allowed therein, and in most cases only if they stipulate more favourable working conditions for employees.

14.2 Employment Protection

[332] The rights of employees are ensured in various ways under Hungarian law: (i) employee representative bodies have the right to be informed and consulted on certain questions; (ii) the employees are granted representation at the supervisory board of the employer; (iii) in the case of a business transfer, the employment contract of the transferring employees stay in place with unchanged terms and conditions; and (iv) special rules apply to the termination of the employment relationship by the employer (e.g., reasons for dismissal) ensuring that employees are not entirely exposed to the discretion of the employer. These rules protecting the employees' rights are mandatory and cannot be altered to the detriment of the employees.

[24] The time spent on the communication with the relevant foreign authorities is disregarded when calculation the procedural deadline.

14.2.1 Protection in the Event of a Business Transfer

[333] In the case of a business transfer, all the employees belonging to the relevant business must be transferred (i.e., no cherry-picking is allowed) with unchanged rights and obligations, and continuity of employment must be preserved.

14.2.2 Employee Representation at Supervisory Board

[334] If the number of full-time employees at a company exceeds 200, a supervisory board must be established, provided that the works council has not waived the right to participate. In such cases, one-third of the members of the supervisory board must be representative(s) of the employees. Such member(s) are delegated by the works council.

14.2.3 Information/Consultation

[335] In some questions the works council has to be informed regularly, e.g., (i) on fundamental issues affecting the employer's financial situation; (ii) on utilization of working time, and the characteristics of working conditions; (iii) trends in wages and salaries, etc. In addition to this, the works council may request information from the employer in respect of any questions that relate to the employees' economic or social interests and the employer cannot reject the request/withhold the information.

[336] Before the employer adopts a decision affecting a large number of employees, consultation is required with the works council in the case of, e.g., (i) a business transfer; (ii) reorganization, transformation, merger, spin-off, mass redundancies; (iii) measures for compliance with occupational safety and health requirements; (iv) the introduction of new work organization methods and performance requirements, etc. However, the works council does not have a right of veto in any of these questions. Furthermore, if there is a trade union at the employer, the trade union can also request information from the employer in any matters relating to the employees and to be consulted in any matters. Similar to the works council, the trade union also has no right of veto. We note that the trade union is entitled to conclude a collective agreement with the employer but collective agreements are typical only at those employers that pursue production/manufacturing activities.

14.2.4 Protection in Relation to the Termination of the Employment Relationship

[337] Indefinite term employment relationships may be terminated either by the employer or the employee by three means: by mutual consent, ordinary notice or extraordinary notice. In addition, special provisions apply to the termination of a fixed-term employment relationship and to a collective redundancy.

[338] Both indefinite and fixed-term employment relationships may be terminated by mutual consent. In that case, the employment relationship ends on the agreed date, which must be included in a written agreement. Furthermore, even the employment of protected employees may be terminated by mutual consent.

[339] Ordinary notice terminates the employment relationship at the end of the notice period. As a general rule, the notice period is a minimum of thirty calendar days but it cannot, in any case, exceed six months. Furthermore, the minimum statutory notice period of thirty calendar days gradually increases in line with the length of the employment at the respective employer if the employment relationship is terminated by the employer, starting from an additional five days after three years' employment up to an extra sixty calendar days (which means a ninety calendar days' notice period) after twenty years of employment at the relevant employer. If the employment relationship is terminated by the employer, employees must be exempted from work for at least half of the notice period.

[340] Ordinary notice of termination must be provided in writing. The employer must provide clear, real, reasonable and proper reasons in the case of the termination of employment by ordinary notice. Such reasons can only be in connection with the employee's ability, conduct related to the employment relationship, and operations of the employer (such as restructuring). No reasons are required to be provided if the employee terminates an indefinite term employment relationship by ordinary notice, except if the employee terminates the employment relationship in the case of a change of the employer (business transfer), claiming that the work conditions have changed substantially and adversely and that this renders the continuation of the employment relationship impossible, or that as a result, the continuation of the employment relationship would cause a disproportionate constraint to him/her.

[341] If the employee's employment relationship is terminated by the employer by ordinary notice, and the service of the employee at the relevant employer has reached or exceeded three years, the employee is entitled to severance payment. The amount of severance payment gradually increases in line with the length of the employment at the respective employer until twenty-five years of employment when the severance payment is six months' average salary. However, the parties may increase this amount. No severance payment needs to be paid to the employee if the reasons for the ordinary notice are based on the conduct of the employee or his/her abilities (excluding health-related abilities).

[342] The employment of employees who are pregnant or on certain leave, such as sick leave, military service, maternity leave, paternity leave or unpaid leave for nursing a child may not be terminated by ordinary notice during such periods of leave.

[343] Employees may turn to the court within thirty calendar days in order to challenge the termination of their employment.

[344] Extraordinary notice terminates the employment relationship with immediate effect (without notice period) and may be applied in very rare cases, such as in the case of a serious breach of the employment contract or if either party's conduct makes the continuation of the employment relationship impossible. Termination by extraordinary notice is possible only in the case of a breach of a material obligation (either intentionally or by gross negligence) or in the case of conduct which makes the continuation of the employment impossible.

[345] As a general rule, both the employer and the employee are obliged to provide appropriate reasons if the employment is terminated in this way. The Labour Code sets out a strict deadline for the exercise of the right to give extraordinary notice, which is fifteen days from becoming aware of the reason for the extraordinary termination. However, in any event, the employment relationship cannot be terminated by extraordinary notice later than one year following the occurrence of the reason (except in the case of a crime, where the extraordinary notice may be exercised until the expiry of the statutory limitation period). Notwithstanding the aforesaid, the employment relationship may be terminated by immediate notice by both the employer and the employee without reason during the probation period, as well as, by the employer in case of a fixed-term employment relationship with simultaneous compensation of the employee.

[346] If the employment relationship is terminated, the employer has to pay the employee's wages and further allowances (e.g., unpaid leave) and it has to hand over to the employee the statutory certificates within five business days following the last day at work or the termination of the employment relationship at the latest.

14.3 Retention of Key Management and Employees

[347] Under Hungarian law, the employee cannot, during the course of his/her employment relationship with his/her employer, engage in a conduct that would threaten the lawful economic interest of his/her employer, i.e., he/she cannot perform work for another employer without the consent of the employer. In order for the employer to be able to prevent an employee from carrying out work for a competitor following the termination of the employment relationship non-competition clauses may be incorporated in the employment contracts or, alternatively, a separate non-competition agreement can be concluded between the parties.

[348] On the basis of such non-competition clause/agreement, within two years following the termination of the employment relationship (for whatever reason), the employee cannot engage in a conduct that would harm or threaten the lawful economic interest of the employer. The employee is entitled to appropriate compensation in respect of such restriction. The amount of the compensation must be at least one-third of the base wage of the employee due for the relevant period affected by the non-competition restriction. The non-competition restriction can only be enforced if the employee is granted the compensation set out by law.

14.3.1 Labour Costs

[349] Hungary is a Member State of the OECD and therefore the tax regulation of foreign employees is generally based on the OECD Model Tax Convention. Pursuant to the Act on PIT the tax liability is based on residence. Resident private individuals are subject to tax in respect of all their income (all-inclusive tax liability).

[350] The tax liability of non-resident private individuals (foreign employees) applies to income that originates in Hungary as the place of gainful activity or is taxable in Hungary by virtue of international agreement or reciprocity (limited tax liability). The Act on PIT provides a long list of conditions relating to the definition of a resident private individual, of which the most important are citizenship or residence in Hungary for 183 days.

[351] The general labour costs are considered to be high despite the fact that the general salaries are below the EU average. There is a generally high tax burden for employers and other obligations concerning taxation procedures. Except for the transportation sector, unions are considered to be weak in Hungary. Collective bargaining agreements are not widespread in the labour market.

[352] The Hungarian pension system is a dual one. Following a reform, most citizens are now in the government pension system but a few have stayed in private pension funds. The pension contribution is paid by the employees.

14.3.2 Liability of Directors (Executive Officers)

[353] The Civil Code regulates the liability of the executive officers (e.g., the managing director of a limited liability company). The major points regarding the liability of the directors are:

- if the director caused the damage deliberately, the director and the company are jointly and severally liable for damages caused to third persons, otherwise, the company is liable for damages caused by the director to third persons;
- in the event of the company's termination without a legal successor, the secondary liability of directors remains, but abates somewhat, as under the Civil Code, the director is liable only if he disregarded the creditors' interests altogether;
- in the case of an onerous contract, a director incurs no liability if he/she proves that the damage was caused by a circumstance that fell outside his control and was unforeseeable at the time of the conclusion of the contract and that he could not have been expected to either evade the circumstance or to prevent the damage;
- if the director's contract is unpaid, in the case of defective performance, the injured party must prove that the director caused the damage through wilful breach, or failed to provide information on an aspect of the subject of the contract that was unknown to the injured party. In case of damage to the assets of the injured party, the director is not liable if he acted as generally expected in the given circumstances.

[354] If the executive officer concerned is engaged through an employment contract and causes damage to his/her employer by a breach of an obligation arising from the employment relationship, the executive officer would be fully liable to pay compensation to the employer for the damage caused.

14.4 Treatment of Foreign Employees

[355] Non-Hungarian citizens can be appointed as executive officers (e.g., managing directors) of Hungarian companies. However, subject to their citizenship, restrictions may apply to their employment and residency in Hungary.

[356] Generally, only citizens of the EU and EEA Member States may work in Hungary without holding a specific residence permit for work purposes. Accordingly, third-county nationals (citizens of non-EU or non-EAA Member States) are required to apply for an appropriate permit for the purpose of gainful employment, the most common forms of which are: (i) residence permit for work purposes; (ii) residence permit for executives and supervisory board members of a Hungarian company with a foreign shareholding; or (iii) intra-corporate transfer permits (ICT permit) where the third-country nationals can be seconded to a Hungarian company belonging to the same group for a period up to three years.

www.ingramcontent.com/pod-product-compliance
Lightning Source LLC
Chambersburg PA
CBHW071356230926
51846CB00002B/572
* 9 7 8 9 4 0 3 5 3 0 9 8 7 *